W9-CQA-911

LET'S GET GROWING

GROWING

[ACT DON'T REACT]

by

Eve Cappello, Ph.D

A Hearthstone Book

Carlton Press, Inc.   New York, N.Y.

To Fran and Alan
my children
my friends
my sources of inspiration

LET'S GET GROWING
(Act Don't React)

A step by step program for developing individual potential using
Behavioral and Assertive techniques. A unique method designed
to build self-esteem and confidence while becoming more
personally effective in everyday living.

by
Eve Cappello Ph.D.

ACKNOWLEDGEMENTS

This is to thank those who encouraged my efforts. Those wonderful people who didn't doubt I could do it even when I had my own doubts. I thank those people closest to me. It is also to acknowledge the hundreds of people who have sat in my classes, listened to my lectures and reinforced what I knew in my heart—the program works. It is a sincere Thank You to all those people who have improved their lives with the A-C-T program and told me time and time again how much it means to them.

A special thanks to Kathy and Bobbie who shortened sentences, deleted commas and read through my scribblings.

Without you, Alan, I would not have been able to accomplish the feat. To you, my son, for all your help and patience, I owe the biggest thanks of all.

Eve Cappello Ph.D.

CONTENTS

FOREWORD

Let's face it, we are all frustrated in some respects. Frustrated because we are aching to tell someone how we feel, and hoping desperately that someone will listen and care. Is it really possible to be rid of the frustration? You bet it is! The important thing to remember, as you read the following pages, is *how* it can be done. Don't waste time worrying about *why* it can't be done. Stand up and be counted!

There are thousands of "How To" books on the market. What makes this one so different? A-C-T DON'T RE-ACT or Let's Get Growing offers a practical method for living and enjoying each day. The A-C-T method has been tested with thousands of people in classes, workshops and seminars. It's a "how can I make the most of today," approach, based on the work of noted psychologists (see references) and my own experiences in working with the public for over twenty years.

The method is unique, in that it is designed to help you, the reader, to have a happier, more fulfilling life without going through the pain to get there. This is accomplished by learning how to overcome the self-defeating behavior that keeps you from acting in your own best interests. It offers a way to use each day more effectively and have more energy and good gut feeling than you dreamed possible. I know it can be done—I live it every day.

It takes a little work, just a few minutes a day, so that feeling good becomes "natural." Follow the chapters one at a time and watch your awareness increase, your confidence grow and your effectiveness improve at home, on the job and in intimate relationships.

With all due respect to programs like est, you don't need someone to tell you how lousy you are. You already know how depressing it is to feel that way. You also don't need someone to give you false hopes, you've had enough disappointments to fill your own book. What you do need, is a sure-fire way to communicate your feelings to other people without groping for the right words. What you need is to be able to speak up, not to let others put you down and generally be more assertive. You need answers here and now!

Chances are, a good portion of your life has already passed you by. The A-C-T method won't help those who are looking for a "cop-out," the people who are saying, "I don't know why this is happening to me," or, "I can't help it, my friends, my loved ones, and my boss won't let me be myself." It's for those who are sick and tired of not being themselves and want to take charge of their own lives by learning to be responsible for their own actions.

Here is a practical approach that can help you realize and develop your own potential. You can live the rest of your life the way you want to by learning how to A-C-T instead of *RE*-ACT.

Welcome to the A-C-T (Assert Consciously Today) Method. Let's Get Growing!

Eve Cappello Ph.D.

LET'S GET GROWING

[ACT DON'T REACT]

CHAPTER I

GETTING TO KNOW YOU

(Getting in Touch with Yourself)

Wouldn't it be great to be able to make decisions when they are needed and stand up for what you believe? Wouldn't it be great to become self-directed and express yourself the way you want to without feeling embarrassed, guilty or ready to crawl into the woodwork and disappear when somebody takes advantage of you? Keep in mind, with each step you accomplish, you are on your way to doing just that—being more self-directed and less anxious.

Getting to know you is learning to become more aware of yourself, your needs and your desires—how you really feel about yourself, your gut feeling. After all, if you can't be honest with yourself, how can you be honest with the people around you?

Think about the snap judgements you make each day, for instance, when you meet other people. Those little "mental notes" you make to yourself about the food you eat, the clothes you wear, the way you enjoy (or don't enjoy) sexual relationships. These judgements or mental notes are clues to the real you. It's important to get in touch with yourself, to start looking at the real you, the person you've hidden under all the "no-nos" and all the fears that have kept you from accepting yourself and making the most of your life. Because it's important to like yourself, get acquainted with the *I Factor.*

The I Factor

The *I Factor* is learning to evaluate and value your own lifestyle. You are going to learn to like yourself gradually and to change the things that frustrate you and cause you anxiety. This is the first step toward self-direction and self-confidence. We are going to start *not* taking ourselves for granted with a simple exercise in awareness. The purpose of the exercise is to increase your awareness about yourself and others. (If you feel embarrassed or silly about this, do it anyway. The embarass-

11

ment will pass once you're involved.) Get together with a friend, your mate, or co-workers, and enjoy a sharing experience. Before you start, read over the steps below. A third party can read the steps aloud s-l-o-w-l-y while the rest of you are increasing awareness. Now let's get growing!

Step 1. Find a comfortable chair and sit *quietly* with your eyes closed for a few moments. Listen to your heartbeat and your breathing. Get in touch with how you feel this moment. There is no yesterday, no tomorrow, only right now. Think about how you feel.

Step 2. Start feeling your hands. Don't pass over them quickly as though they belong to someone else. Feel the fingers, the knuckles, the nails, etc. Think about how your hands feel to you. Take your time, you are going to like yourself more than you ever have.

Step 3. Now feel your head (where did that bump come from?) Run your fingers lightly over your closed eyes, cheeks, nose, lips and chin. Feel how different each part feels, as well as the different sensations you are experiencing.

Step 4. Now with your eyes still closed and still not talking, reach out and take the other person's hand. Allow yourself to feel the hand and hold it.

Step 5. Open your eyes and look at each other closely (even if your mother told you it's not polite to stare). Think about your gut-level reaction.

Step 6. Now—discuss with each other what it felt like to touch yourself and then each other. How does it feel to share your feelings with someone else? Sharing your experience with another person is developing your communication skills. If it felt good, talk about it (talk about it even if it felt weird). Express your own worth and feel the worth of someone else. If you can do this with one person, it can be done with groups and eventually warm feelings can be shared with entire cultures. You didn't realize what an important contribution you can make to humanity. You and your feelings are important. Don't ever forget it. Pat each other on the back and shake hands. You deserve to thank each other and feel good about starting to *act*, in spite of any embarrassment you might have experienced before the exercise. (This is great to practice on your lunch hour with your co-workers. It will bring you closer and save you money because you didn't run out shopping.)

Now that you've had some experience practicing communication skills, you may as well know that actions often do speak louder than words. We often communicate more of what we mean to others with something commonly called *body language.* This is a nonverbal behavior that can give you and others more insight into what is being said than the words themselves communicate. For example, you can usually tell when someone is angry (the voice is often a dead giveaway), even if he says, "No, that doesn't bother me." Now you know damn well it bothers him and maybe you even begin to feel like, "Oh, oh, what did I do to make him angry?"

Body language is often more important to the messages we convey than the actual words we use. Body language is *how* we put the message across, the way we use our eyes, the tone of voice, our hands, etc. It gives us clues to what a person really means. Body language is often subtle, mostly hidden and often delivered without awareness; but sometimes it has an astounding ability to control others. For example, raising your voice in anger is one of the fastest ways to get someone involved with you and get a reaction. A good way to increase awareness of body language is to pay closer attention to *how* people say things. Do they have eye contact with you when they speak, or do they avoid looking at you directly? Is their speaking voice rapid, shrill? Are theirs hands relaxed or do they show signs of nervous movement. (If the reader wants to pursue the art of body language further, please see references.) A word of caution here, even when you think you can 'read' what someone means by the visible and audible (overt) messages they are sending out to you, it's usually wiser and more assertive to ask them what they mean, rather than to tell them you got their message. They may become defensive if you accuse them of meaning something different from what their words indicated. Even if you are right, they may be defensive or angry at your insight! Tread lightly. Because you have ammunition and know how to pull the trigger doesn't mean you shoot everyone in sight. Assertive people consider others and allow them to save face. (More about Assertiveness later.)

Practicing Self-Acceptance

Now that you are getting to know you, it is important to get to like you. You can start by eliminating negative images about yourself. Don't tell yourself you are an awful or terrible person if you do something you don't like or make a mistake. When you tell yourself how bad you are, that image of 'awfulness' is difficult to overcome. Eliminate the negative imagery by replacing that kind of thinking with thoughts of things you like about yourself. Kick the habit of putting yourself down. Start practicing now!

Think of a booboo you made where you not only criticized yourself, but maybe received negative criticism from others as well, something that made you feel guilty, embarassed, or klutzy. When you made the booboo, chances are you were harder on yourself than anyone else could ever be. You may have even wasted such precious energy being so hard on yourself, that you weren't capable of handling other situations in your life. Don't punish yourself. It drives you further into what you were castigating yourself about in the first place and it immobilizes you so you can't act. *Act, Don't React!*

Face it and deal with it. You did it, now go on and live your life. It is human to act undesirably from time to time. Who says you are under obligation to do the right thing all the time? Practice saying, "OK, I goofed" or some similar phrase, to free you from that lifelong habit of thinking you are a terrible person because you goofed. The practice will help free you from embarrasment and guilt. (Assertive people don't put themselves down.) Would it be earth shattering for you if you began to accept yourself as less than perfect? It's time to turn away from the preoccupations of discomfort and begin to search for comfortable feelings within ourselves.

In addition to practicing saying "OK, I goofed." you can build self-acceptance by taking a good look at the "shoulds" you allow to control your life. "You *should* be a good girl, *should* get married, *should* respect your elders," and on and on. Now I'm not suggesting you shouldn't be a good girl (whatever that is), shouldn't get married, etc. What I am suggesting is, you make sure those "shoulds" you live by are *your* values and not someone else's. If you start feeling guilty, have knots in your stomach, get uptight when you give in compulsively to a "should" (maybe you don't really feel up to doing something for someone else today, but you do it because you've been taught you shouldn't say no), those are pretty good indications for you to start eliminating some of those "shoulds," or at least decreasing them from your daily existence. After all, when you are living by what you "should" be doing a great deal of the time instead of what you *could* be doing, where does that leave you?

Practice saying "I can function efficiently and happily in spite of the 'shoulds' and negative feelings I've been hanging onto all these years." You can't go back and change what it was that made you feel badly in the first place, but you can challenge those negative feelings by *consciously* and *deliberately* choosing an action that gives you good feelings instead. When you begin to choose positives, the negatives will change.

The Fun Jar

Remember earlier I said that growing doesn't have to be painful? Here's a painless and fun way to help you out of a funk. Somewhere handy, keep a piece of paper and jot down things you really like to do for yourself—go to a movie, get a massage, take a bubble bath, whatever. Be inventive. Jot down those things you've promised yourself, but never got around to doing. You don't have to come up with the list all at once, but do add to the list from time to time. Remember everything has to be enjoyable—that's what the Fun Jar is all about. Now, when you have about a dozen things you like to do for YOU, cut the list into strips of paper so that each strip has one item on it. Fold each strip in half and put the strips into a jar or container. When you are feeling low or depressed, reach in and take out one of the things to do for yourself and *do it!* Don't make excuses and say "I don't feel like it," etc., etc. Of course you don't feel like it! By consciously and deliberately choosing and doing an enjoyable or pleasing experience, the funk or depression will disappear.

Some of my students have really become involved with this project by decorating their Fun Jars in ingenious ways. One of the fringe benefits that has evolved from the use of the jar is, I am told, the pleasure of knowing you are going to select something enjoyable is increased by the anticipation of not knowing *which* pleasurable thing you are going to select. "Ah, sweet mystery of life. . ." In the search for self-acceptance and self-fulfillment, you don't have to feel guilty if you are good to yourself occasionally. It's OK—enjoy!

Speaking of enjoying yourself, it isn't always feasible to walk away from the job or change the environment when the pressures build up, but you can relieve some of the tension with a little practice exercise in Imagery, wherever you are. Because offices, walls and indoor environments are generally confining, physically, as well as mentally, let's take an imaginary trip outdoors for a few moments. (If you want to be alone, you can always go to the john or the broom closet.) Close your eyes and imagine yourself in a beautiful grassy area, maybe with a sparkling ocean or lake nearby. Let your imagination take over. What kind of day is it? Is it sunny, is there a breeze, are there flowers? Maybe there's a hill you feel like climbing. Start running (in your imagination, of course, not in the broom closet) and feel the wind in your hair, the freedom of outdoors. Feel how good it is to be alive. When you have run until you are tired(remember, you do have to get back, so don't spend the day in the broom closet), open your eyes, take a couple of deep breaths and stretch. Now you can go back and tackle what you have to. Feeling good will help you approach and complete your daily work, despite the everpresent pressures. Feeling good can even help you to learn to live more easily with the mistakes you are bound to make. Practice feeling good.

Speaking of mistakes, we all know the old cliche, "to err is human." What we fail to realize sometimes is that errors are not necessarily failures. Inventions would never be invented without the learner's willingness to try, to risk, to discover and create. Now don't tell yourself that it is easy for me to say. Remember, we're in this thing together. Trial and error ultimately point the way to successful results. You are going to grow and like it—so let yourself grow!

Allow yourself to feel—even if it's sad or disappointed. You have all kinds of feelings, so sweeping them under the rug won't help get rid of them. Thank your lucky stars you are a feeling, thinking, alive human being, and accept the fact that all your feelings aren't the greatest that life has to offer. When you're dead, you can stop feeling (even *that* is debatable). When those feelings do get you down, start thinking about what you can do to help yourself feel better. Maybe you slipped off your diet and were really angry at yourself. Say to yourself, "I feel pretty crummy about this right now," and let it go at that. Negative feelings can motivate you to try harder sometimes. Replace that negative with a positive and think of something better to do. *Do It Now!* Even if you run around the block to burn off the calories, that is better than beating yourself to death because you ate too much and are trying to "understand why you did it."

Alternatives

Running around the block is only one option. You may think of others. Always think options in situations, not just one or two ways, especially in situations that give you anxiety or guilt. Sometimes, the best way to cope with a problem is to think of as many possible options as fast as you can and choose the best one to handle the situation at hand. The one best way changes in every situation. "How many different ways can I think of?" will make the difference between dwelling on negatives and thinking positives. When you think in terms of either/or, you are at the extremes of a situation. Being at the extremes limits your actions as well as your thinking. It only gives you two alternatives. Neither one may be the answer for you.

How to Use Rationalization

Where does it say you should be a smashing success? Don't expect the impossible. Sometimes society sets standards you are miserable trying to live up to. The depression, the guilt is all too familiar to all of us when we start dwelling on what we think we "should" have done. Talk to yourself and challenge the "shoulds." Ask yourself, "who says I should have," then the depressed feelings will be on the way out. Challenging the "shoulds" will not only increase your self-awareness but may even pleasantly surprise you in building your own self-esteem. (Your self-esteem could use a little boost.)

A-C-T: Risk-Taking

Getting into new situations, especially ones that involve you personally, like giving up old frustrating but familiar habits, is a little like going swimming in unheated water. Once you're in the water, it's comfortable. Getting there is half the agony. Getting there without agony or discomfort comes with learning and practice. You even begin to feel new surges of energy and confidence as new patterns of self-satisfying and effective behavior become a part of everyday living. Does the thought of speaking up or expressing an opinion hold terrors for you? Are you painfully shy? Are you one of those who wish you could say what's on your mind instead of feeling the pain of frustration? Here's one option for getting over the loneliness

17

and the anxiety. You can use this guideline whether it's at a party with unfamiliar people or asking your boss for a raise. If other people terrify you, look at it this way—*they* aren't really terrifying you, now are they? Aren't *you* the one who is scared to speak up?

Force yourself to speak up, at least to start the conversation where you might normally hold back. Start putting the anxiety in its place (like over to one side) and ask a question, especially in social situations, just to start the ball rolling. Ask open-ended questions, not questions that elicit a straight "yes or no" answer. Get involved. For example, an open-ended question would be, "What do you like about this book, lecture, painting, etc.?" rather than, "Do you like it?" The "Do you like it" leads to a dead end of "yes" or "no." The open-ended question can lead to further conversation, whether it is directed at one person or a group. The object is to get to know someone better and at the same time help you rid yourself of anxiety with strangers.

You can ask someone, "Have you travelled? Where? When?" "What's it like?" If you haven't been there, or you may share similar experiences if you have. You can even say to someone, "You look like a person I'd like to meet." That's bound to get a response. Don't hold back and be afraid to approach someone, even your boss, if you have what *you* think is a good idea.

If starting the conversation makes you anxious, admit it. You can say, "I'm learning to overcome it. Have you ever felt that way? I have an idea, opinion about that..." and express it. Admitting your anxiety will lessen it. Don't expect yourself to be a brilliant conversationalist at all times. Hang in there. The more you practice, the more your conversations will develop. The more they develop, the better you will feel about yourself. You can also ask questions to get the other person talking. Become a good listener!

If the other party appears uninterested (only the other person knows for sure), keep trying with others. Don't tell yourself, "See, it didn't work, I knew it, and on and on." The other person may have anxieties also. With practice, you can get yourself to change that shy, non-assertive behavior that prevents you from interacting with others and having good feelings about yourself.

Practicing is important, I can't stress this point enough. You need to practice, not only with yourself, but with others as well. Before you try the new behaviors on your mate, your boss, your children or friends, practice with others not involved in the anxious situation. Corner a friend over lunch and say, "hey, I'm reading this book that just might help me overcome my anxiety and I need your help. My name is. . .(sure they know your name, but you are practicing, remember?) and I don't know anyone here. I'd like to get to meet you. Can you introduce me to others?" and so on. You may feel a little embarrassed at first but express it. Say, "I'm a little embarrassed doing this, but I do want to get past that." Involve your friends.

A general problem most people share is anxiety in a new situation. Whether it's meeting new people or speaking up in situations, you may have suppressed your feelings previously and then resented yourself because you did. By practicing, the situation becomes more familiar and less anxious. Treat yourself to the luxury of expressing yourself the way you've always wanted to. Meeting others can be not only painless, it can be fun. Later there will be more specific skills to practice to make you even more effective. Watch out world—here you come!

FIRST WEEK ASSIGNMENT

Note: Assignments are to be carried out in real life situations, in stores, in offices, with your mechanic etc. The assignments can be fun, but the purpose is serious and essential to the method. Get Growing!

  A. Start on the Fun Jar.
  B. Think of different ways to initiate conversations with strangers, friends and relatives (the weather is already exhausted). Force yourself to initiate, continue and conclude a five minute conversation with someone you ordinarily wouldn't be talking to. If you have trouble ending the conversation without sounding awkward, say, "I'm glad we talked, I enjoyed it." (Something positive you did like.) Shake hands, touch, hug, smile and say, "goodbye, that's all I have time for, when can I see you?" (if you want to see them again) and *leave.* It's Time to Get Growing!

CHAPTER 2

PINPOINTING FEELINGS

How did you feel when you started practicing some of the things we talked about in Chapter 1? Did the unfamiliar become more familiar and consequently less anxious as you repeated it? Yes, *you* actually made it happen and I'll bet you didn't think you could do it. The more familiar a situation becomes, the easier and less threatening it is. Did you find that expressing your anxiety helped reduce it? The worst didn't happen, did it? Even if you think you bungled the whole thing, you made it, you're here and you can learn to equip yourself so that the next situation can be handled more smoothly.

Pinpointing Feelings

So that you can handle situtations more effectively, it is important to take a good look at the way you handle them already. Now don't start getting self-conscious. After all, this is only for your own information, so you can function the way you've always wanted to. You don't have to advertise what you think are your shortcomings. You may even be able to turn those "shortcomings" into assets with a little modification. Honest appraisal is getting to know *you* and then learning what to do with what you've got.

Start thinking about specific situations in which you wish you were more assertive; for example, asking for a date, asking for sex (saying yes when you want to say yes), refusing sex (not just giving in because your partner thinks you should), going to new places alone, or meeting strangers. Once you pinpoint the situation, you can learn how to handle it.

Let's say you are going to enter a room filled with strangers and the act is a one-time situation and you are experiencing anxiety. First, on entering the room, think about actions, not feelings (it comes with *practice*—there's that word again!). Observe the people and their behavior, both verbal and non-verbal. Pay attention to the body language. It does convey a message, remember? Be Consciously Aware. Exercise control (you can do it), and don't let the anxiety take over. Think about who you will talk to and what you will say. Don't spend time and energy worrying about your anxiety. Who needs it? Concentrate on the people. You do need them.

For a moment now, let's think about the emotional selections you usually make, people you think you ordinarily want to meet. More often then not, that kind of thinking is based on prejudice, conditioning, even someone you think you may feel comfortable with. This kind of selectivity is too narrow. You miss out on many rewarding relationships. Consider the options you ordinarily choose: black, white, short, tall, blond, or handsome—the things you usually use as criteria before you actually make contact. Sometimes we single out people because they turn us on sexually or they remind us of someone we once knew. This doesn't give you a broad enough social environment. It may even push you into repeating the same old unrewarding, self-defeating mistakes.

Do the opposite—select differently, try another alternative. Open yourself up to more than one kind of experience, even if that experience doesn't turn out to be the greatest. Pre-judging narrows your experiences, and you are going to grow, remember? If the experience is not to your liking, you don't have to pursue the relationship. Do permit yourself the experience. You may even be pleasantly surprised.

Practice! (there it is again). You'll read that word so often you'll probably start making faces at the book. Go ahead, make faces, but it takes practice to get to a point, at which, no matter what or who tries to hold you back, you can ACT constructively pursue your basic values, your goals and the happiness that makes your life more meaningful. By practice, you are modifying or changing the anxious behavior to behavior that minimizes your anxieties and makes your life more satisfying. Strive for positive action!

Rating the Deed

Do you ever feel guilty over something you've said or done, maybe even something you haven't done (but feel you "should")? Don't rate yourself, rate the deed. For example, suppose you yelled at your child in anger and it wasn't the child's fault. It is okay to level with the child and say, "I yelled at you because I was angry about something else and I'm sorry I took it out on you." At least the other person can understand what is happening when you level with him or her. You might even gain a whole new respect for each other. Remember, if you do something wrong, it doesn't make you a wrong person. Don't lay that on yourself and don't waste precious energy on guilt. Start accepting yourself as human and let others in on the secret too.

You may not have complete free will, there may be some social or biological restrictions, but you do have a great deal of determinism and choice. Start exercising it! We are conditioned that there are only certain ways to do things. That's not necessarily true. We get locked into behavior patterns, not necessarily because they are a better way to do things, but because we get used to them. We are creatures of habit. It's easier to repeat habits (positive or negative). However, the same old familiar habits don't always make you happier or more effective.

Frustrating and unfulfilling habits, no matter how long they have been a part of you, can be replaced with new behaviors and practiced until the new habits become natural. If you don't believe it, ask someone who indulged himself with rich foods all his life, had a heart attack and then became cholesterol conscious. The choice is yours. Look for other options, other ways to make your life more fulfilling. You will find there is usually more than one way to do things even if you don't thing so at the moment. Don't be afraid to try out those options. If they don't work, look for other options. Kick the habits and patterns that you get feeling uptight. You deserve to feel good!

Practicing Risks

If one of your habits is holding back when you meet new people, letting anxiety and shyness take hold of you because you fear rejection, learn how to handle it. Don't just give up and say, "That's the way I am." It's not the way you are. It's the way you've learned to be, for whatever reasons. The reasons for being anxious are not important. What is important, is changing your behavior and learning to feel freer. Once you see yourself making more positive moves, the more confident and less anxious you'll be. Don't take this statement on faith. Try it out for yourself.

Social risk-taking is not as horrifying as you've imagined. Teach yourself to approach someone by repeating successful behavior or learning new ways. Say you do apporach someone and you get no response. So what? It's not the end of the world. Try someone else or another approach until you polish your performance. The important thing is to keep trying and build communication skills while you build confidence.

What if you really try your wings and get up the nerve to ask your mate or lover to go to bed with you and he or she says, "Not tonight, honey, I've got a headache and I'm tired." Okay, it bothers you, but don't magnify this "no" out of all proportion. Don't treat it as a huge rejection and allow yourself to get depressed looking for things wrong with *you*. Look at it for what it is—only *one* turn down. Big deal! If you want to, you can choose to initiate a different action with the same person (they may even get rid of the headache), or choose to try that same approach with a different person. (After all, one man's meat. . .as the saying goes.)

The point is, if someone turns you down after you've taken the risk of initiating new behavior and stuck your neck out, there will be a risk of not getting everything you wanted. Think of how much freer you will feel taking that risk, especially if you were too shy to risk it in the first place. Don't let one disappointment control you and stop you from acting. Learn not to expect one-hundred percent and examine what you can do to increase the percentage you are getting now.

Things, like habits (positive or negative ones) that you've learned to do in your life, have been reinforced, otherwise you wouldn't keep them as part of your behavior. When you get approval or positive feedback for a particular behavior, you more than likely will repeat that behavior. Since we like approval, we tend to repeat those actions that receive it. When this kind of approval increases the frequency of that behavior, it is called Social Reinforcement.

Positive reinforcement in the forms of praise, applause, pats on the back, etc., let us know how well we've performed. We like to think we continue only positive behavior. However, we do keep negative behavior patterns even when they have had negative reinforcement. For example, maybe one or both parents slapped you or yelled at you when you were a child. Even though you knew your actions would get a negative response, perhaps a painful and unpleasant one, you still continued to repeat that behavior. Perhaps that kind of attention was better for you than no attention at all. Therefore, you became accustomed to behaving in a specific way to get the attention you needed and wanted. You don't need to hang on to that kind of behavior and its limitations. You are no longer a child.

We've also accepted role limitations. If you are male, you've been given the whole *macho* image. Be aggressive, be the breadwinner, don't be a sissy, etc. Scripts are written for us and we are supposed to act them out without question. When we do question, *we* are the oddballs, *they* are correct. If females want to learn to fix their cars, ask for a date, or be less dependent, it's okay to do so. It's even okay for men to cry and putter in the kitchen. Do what makes you feel good.

The behaviors and attitudes that accompany role limitations change with practice. Some attitudes regarding the male/female roles are changing, but attitudes die hard. Behaviors must be practiced and reinforced before they seem natural to you. What seems natural to you now, wasn't at one time in your life. It had to be learned. You can shape your own behavior. Start shaping!

Shaping Behavior

This is a technique that can be used to achieve more successful communication in interpersonal relationships. Shaping means that frequent approval is given for each successful attempt. Say that your husband poops out in front of the TV set after dinner and doesn't talk to you. The only time he opens his mouth is to stuff it with popcorn or say "Let's go to bed, it's getting late." Now this can be frustrating, especially if you've been at home all day. Nagging him only makes him resentful or less talkative and you more frustrated, so nothing is really accomplished. What you want to do is encourage some conversation.

To get some conversation going, use the positive approach. Ask him some open-ended questions. Tell him (or her) you'd like some suggestions for a picnic, marriage encounter, switching partners or whatever might interest you both. When he or she does reply, encourage that kind of behavior by reaching out (or walking over) and planting a big kiss where it will do the most good. Say "I love when you show interest in me that way, you keep it up and I might. . . ." (use your imagination). *That* is shaping behavior, giving frequent approval for successfully better attempts of verbal as well as non-verbal behavior. *Any* sign of improvement is *clearly*, *immediately* and *specifically* praised ("I *love* when you rub my back, etc.").

You can shape and reinforce your own behavior by focusing on the things you say and do well, those things that get you the results you want, e.g., more comfortable feelings or closer contacts. It encourages you and your partner to try again to repeat the successes. If someone criticizes you for a specific behavior, you are not likely to repeat it around the person who does the criticizing.

If you want to be able to help yourself to concentrate on positive reinforcement and shape behavior to have more rewarding relationships, then be aware that behavior rehearsal is the core and framework for learning to be personally effective. Behavior rehearsal differs from therapies like group encounter or psychodrama. Behavior rehearsal emphasizes goal oriented, verbal and non-verbal behavior rather than feelings. What the A-C-T method is saying in essence is: Let's practice the behavior, build confidence, work toward goals in positive and constructive ways, and then enjoy the desirable and good feelings that come from accomplishment. Don't wait until you feel like doing something. Sometimes when you play the game of waiting around for luck to change, anxieties to disappear, your mate to stop pooping out in front of the TV, you build more resentment. Less communication and wider gaps may develop in the relationship. He may not even say "Let's go." Don't wait for luck to happen. Give it a little push. You want to start feeling good, don't you?

Let's have a little dry run to practice some behavior rehearsal. Select an unfamiliar person with whom you can initiate a conversation. Find out his/her name, where they are from, schooling, hobby, a peak experience and goals. This is an easy format to memorize and have handy when you meet new people. It should give you plenty to talk about for awhile. Share similar experiences. You don't have to go into a lengthy spiel about each category. Give each other an opportunity to know whether you have common interests and want to pursue the relationship. If you run out of conversation and want to leave, it's okay to say, "I enjoyed talking with you, but I'm all talked out," and leave. If you want to stay with the person longer, tell him you've run out of things to say and you feel awkward when there is a long silence. Ask him if he ever feels that way. Then the both of you are involved in a whole new conversation.

If you haven't noticed already, "work" as a topic of conversation has been specifically eliminated from the list for this reason, know a person as a human being first before you find out what they do for a living and stereotype them. ("Oh," with eyebrows pushed up to the hairline, "You're an entertainer, hmm.") If you are in a group and single someone out on the opposite side of the room to initiate a conversation, smile as you pass others. Say "Hi" and generally practice being friendly. Concentrate on what you will say and do instead of, "Wow, I wish I could get over being shy." Share your feelings as well as the information. Enjoy the discovery of opening up and listening to people you wouldn't ordinarily engage in conversation.

Think about what specific changes in your behavior might allow you to succeed. That is called Targeting Your Behavior. Start identifying the problem or the anxiety to change particular patterns that prevent you from acting the way you'd like to act. The idea is to change those behaviors that are unrewarding and unfulfilling. In other words, change the behaviors and patterns that give you difficulty.

Before you charge off into a risky situation, decide *what* you'd like to change, *where* you'd like to change and *with whom* you'd like to change it. When you've decided that, write it down and being to practice.

SECOND WEEK ASSIGNMENT

A. Use Imagery. Imagine yourself saying the things you wish you could say to another person. (It works better with your eyes closed.) Keep repeating the image until you feel at ease with the "picture." Work on Imagery daily. Think about what you will say. Visualize positive body language, i.e., standing tall, shoulders erect and voice confident. Don't see yourself as shrinking into the woodwork. Imagery is one of the most effective tools you can use. Use it confidently!

B. Write out or tape your new behavior and familiarize yourself with it. Memorize it if necessary so you won't have to fish for words when you do take the plunge.

C. Try out your new behavior with a sympathetic friend or relative. Tell them what you are practicing, what you are trying to accomplish and tell them you need their help and support. Ask someone who will listen.

D. Talk about your anxiety in the target situation and ask another person how they feel in similar situations. (We don't usually talk about these situations to others for fear they will ridicule us.)

E. Try out a situation (asking for a date, a raise etc.) after you have practiced feeling at ease (with Imagery, etc.). Do try a situation that will be low-risk at first. For example, try out your new behaviors with people not involved in the highly anxious situations. Try situations that are only slightly anxious.

Don't try to make a major overhaul all at once. Concentrate on one specific situation at a time. Build your self-esteem gradually. When you see yourself handling low-risk situations more effectively than before, you will build a strong foundation of verbal and nonverbal skills while building your self-esteem. Allow yourself to enjoy the experience as well as your performance.

Act confidently and you'll feel confident. Act afraid and you'll be afraid. You *feel* the way you *act*—not the reverse. There is nothing insincere or phony in learning to be more effective.

A good way to check yourself to see if you are really changing unacceptable behavior in a goal-oriented, constructive way is to ask yourself:

1. Did I target the specific behavior I want to change?
2. Did I actually change it? How? (What did I say, do, etc?)
3. Did my involvement increase as I practiced?
4. Was it difficult for me to give positive feedback to somone else?
5. What were my reactions to the situation (using the new skills)?
6. Did I see uses for it, that is, was it/is it practical?

With each increase in awareness, you are opening your eyes to a whole new, wonderful way of life. Smile at yourself in the mirror (you devil you, you are going to grow) and let's get growing!

CHAPTER 3

SOCIAL GOAL-SETTING

Now that you are beginning to know who you are, with whom problems exist, and how to identify anxious situations, you can start looking at *where you are headed.* Maybe you've learned that you need to be able to speak up on the job, talk less rapidly, or lower your speaking voice. Whatever the problem is that you have targeted, you need to plan what to do to eliminate the problem or lessen your anxiety or both. Setting a goal is the first step in achieving it.

Importance of Goal-Setting

We all have goals. Even small goals count. Little successes will build self-confidence. You know the good feelings you have when you accomplish something? Well, there are ways to increase those good feelings. Set yourself some small goals at first. It is important to set goals that have some degree of achievability. You might try for better communication with the opposite sex, a more responsible position, more honesty in intimate relationships, etc. Long range goals are great to strive for, but build your confidence by setting goals that are realistic, smaller goals you can achieve in a reasonable amount of time, If you are not sure whether your goals are realistic or idealistic, a good way to test yourself is to write them down and ask yourself (1) Are my goals achievable? (Is it possible for me to go back to college and get that Ph.D.?) (2) Are they realistic? (Do I have enough money or time? Will I be willing to give up other things to get that degree?) (3) Are they functional in my *real* world, that is, the environment I function in with my mate, children, co-workers etc. If the goals aren't practical for your own special environment, they aren't realistic. (Unless of course you intend to change your environment, leave town, family, etc.) Write your goals down daily, even if they are only errands you wish to accomplish that day and check them off as they are completed. This will help you to get your thoughts organized and give you a sense of accomplishment as you go down the list and check off the completed tasks. (Even going to the grocery counts.) Make the goals specific enough to permit direct planning and action. For example, if you are going to build a bookcase, list *all* the items you will need so that once you've determined what they are, you can purchase materials and begin building efficiently without wasting time and energy in making several trips to the store. This applies to everything from going back to school to graduate, to having a dinner party. Plan which action or actions are necessary to achieve the end result.

If you've thought about several areas in which you'd like to change behavior, select one goal at this time that you would like to achieve (start slowly, one at a time, after all you don't want to change the whole you). The goal may be speaking in front of a group, arranging a date, or expressing your opinion in conversation where you might normally hold back. Choose as a target or goal, behaviors which occur at a fairly frequent rate in your life and which, if you could perform effectively or improve upon, would lead to social reward. In other words, if you frequently have to speak to co-workers as a group—a situation in which you are not as skilled as you'd like to be—if the anxiety gets you so uptight you sweat and have a shaky voice, then gaining control of your voice, learning and practicing verbal skills would be more effective for you. Focus directly on your needs and interests when you select a goal.

When we discuss goals in classes, we follow the discussion with role-playing. Role-playing is "acting out" the kind of behavior one *could* use to function more effectively. Rehearsal of how we *could* handle a situation, as opposed to how we already handle it. We usually break up into groups of three in which two people role-play and the third person concentrates on the specific behaviors of each of the others in the group, paying close attention to overt behavior (body language as well as words). The observer's role is to give specific feedback to the others, a) what was done well and, b) what can be improved (eye contact, voice volume, etc.). The feedback is to be positive so as to reinforce what is being done effectively and strengthen what could be more effective. No put-down criticism is allowed. The objective is improvement.

If you can enlist the aid of someone who can stick to the rules, so much the better. However, it has been my experience, as well as the experience of many of my clients, that close friends and relatives will often say you are doing fine, just the way you are. They are often afraid of hurting your feelings. Constructive and positive criticism can be most helpful, e.g., "you put things so well, your choice of words is excellent; however I think you might be more effective if you raised your voice a little so we can hear you better." The classroom or private counsel situation is more conducive to practicing until weaknesses become strengths. When those strengths are practiced often enough to become natural behavior, then you are ready for the big-time. You are then ready to take on situations and handle them effectively without trusting to luck and letting anxiety take over. You don't have to waste precious time worrying how you are going to come out. Skill is the name of the game.

In order to increase your awarness and organize your thoughts regarding goals, here are some of the clues you might follow:

1. Awareness of the situations. That is, *what* situations give me anxiety;
2. What are my gut feelings besides anxiety?
3. What is my *overt* behavior? (What am I doing and saying in the situation?) Looking at the actual overt behavior is separate from thoughts and feelings, which are covert or hidden. Paying attention to the overt (visible and audible behavior) gives you precise behaviors to change, if necesaary.
4. What are my options for change?
5. What are my objectives?

To assess whether you are headed in the right direction, (right for you, that is) ask yourself, what was done well and what specifics could be improved in order for you to handle the situation more effectively the next time something similar arises. By observing you and your behavior more closely, you will be more aware of how to change what isn't working well for you.

Strategy

To achieve the goals we set for ourselves, it is evident that we must develop some system of change, one that really focuses on all the best possible ways to achieve what we want. If it is a new job you are seeking, develop a strategy or plan of attack that will put your plans to work, e.g., revising your resume, learning all you can about the job. Write down the steps necessary in planning your strategy so you will have something concrete to work with. Take the time to be prepared.

To achieve behavioral goals or behavioral change, your plan would include rectifying deficits in your performance by strengthening desirable behaviors, such as toning down overly emotional ways of expressing yourself, like repetition, loud talking, repeated throat clearing, that might turn off others.

Cycle of Successes

Successes that work for you are the ones that bear repeating. If you find you like the way you handle a particular communication or situation, keep it up! It may only need a slight modification when you want to use it with another person, but use it. Never knock success! Having successful interaction builds your self-esteem and your confidence as well as accomplishes what you want to achieve in the first place.

Key Phrases

Let's take a realistic look at words or phrases we all use, words that either kill or encourage incentive. Let's say you want a specific job done around the house and the person you asked has procrastinated so long that you are frustrated about the whole situation. What can you do short of releasing your anger by nagging or exploding?

Instead of using angry or kill words, you can tell the other person how frustrated *you* are (not, "You make me frustrated, it's all your fault."). Ask the person if he still intends to help you and get a definite commitment as to when you can expect the job to be completed. Set a deadline. Don't be trapped into an argument. Stay cool and repeat your feelings and expectations in a low voice. If you get angry and lose track of the issue, you'll have the same old frustration plus anger with yourself for getting angry. You don't need the frustration.

If they still don't do the job, you can either do it yourself or make arrangements for someone else to do it. You don't have to hang on to the frustration. If the first person you asked gets angry because you didn't wait for him or her, you can say, "I felt I waited long enough," (keep cool) and let it go at that. Again, stay out of the other person's anger.

Maybe some of the words you use kill the other person's incentive for doing things. Instead of "Why don't you. . .?" (you'll get a whole list of answers why they can't or shouldn't), ask, "How can we get this done, achieve this, etc.?" *How can we*, focuses on the issue or content of the communication. It is a way of defusing anger and saying, "We are both in this together." That is better than going around in circles with an argument. Some kill words we use are, "You promised" (said in a whining tone), "You *always* do this to me, I can *never* rely on you." Kill words only aggravate an already aggravating situation.

Try to think of encouraging or incentive words, such as, "I asked you because I like the way you do that," or You know more about that than most people I know." You can think up some good incentive words yourself. Stretch your imagination and look for positive statements. Be aware of the sounds or things you do that turn others off (or turn them on), like gum-cracking, blowing smoke in someone's face, drumming fingers on the table. If a person drums his fingers while he is talking to you and it annoys you, ask him not to. Tell him it distracts you from listening to him and that you want to pay close attention to what he is saying. (Keep your voice pleasant and *smile.*)

Turn-offs/Turn-ons

We are so afraid to tell people what turns us off or on. We are afraid they won't approve or may get angry. If someone is habitually late and it annoys the hell out of you, how about saying, "I get turned off when you're late and I don't want to be turned off. Time with you is both enjoyable and precious. I like spending all the time with you I can." (You don't have to be phony or use these exact words, but *do* express your feelings and what you *would* like.)

When we seek approval by not telling the other person how we really feel, we have anxieties which usually stand in the way

32

of a pleasant encounter or good communication. Anxieties in situations often stem from not being honest with another person or ourselves and we get turned off. It is extremely important to get used to not worrying about approval. It is more important to level about feelings in personal relationships, both social and sexual. It takes some getting used to. We've been conditioned to say and do things for approval. Approving of yourself is a big step forward.

How you say something is important. Try to be pleasant. Work on keeping cool when you express your feelings and grow, grow, grow. Be honest with yourself and use the positive things to modify your own behavior to bring about these behaviorial goals. You want to be happier, don't you?

Think about the people you listen to. What is it about *that* person that holds your interest? Use similar successes to achieve your own goals. That is called *modeling.* Using modeling, model your own behavior after the success of others, finding your own unique style and the words you are comfortable with. Modeling is an effective tool. It is copying success.

Flexibility

If your goals are not achieved, maybe you need to change or reappraise them in a more realistic way. If a goal doesn't work, don't be afraid to change it and be flexible. Learn from it and examine what changes might be necessary to make it work. We like to think of ourselves as being flexible, but the truth of the matter is, we are pretty set in our ways. *Not* achieving a goal can be used as a learning experience to review errors, change your strategy or plan differently. There's more than one way, remember?

When you've decided what you really want to do, when you've written it down and started working on it, break it down into components where you can function best, that is, whatever approach you will be most comfortable with in asking for the raise, developing a sexual relationship, whatever. Backing up to where you can function effectively can be a learning experience in itself. It gives you time to gather your forces and prepare yourself for control of your own actions. Don't let the "backing up" throw you for a loop. We all need to take time occasionally to reevaluate, add new input and increase awareness. You may need to buy a little time just to feel less pressured into making a hurried decision or solving a problem. Take the pressure off.

THIRD WEEK ASSIGNMENT

Make a list of your cycle of successes. This can be positive incentive words, phrases of encouragement or sentences that achieve what you want and make you feel good about yourself. Keep the list (and phrases) short and uncomplicated.

Write down a behavioral goal. Make it realistic so it is achievable. For example, speaking in front of a group, speaking less rapidly, not losing your temper with your mother-in-law, etc. List the options you have for achieving that goal. What would you have to do to achieve it? Now *Grow* on from here.

CHAPTER 4

THE BIG "T"

All your life you've lived with tension in some form or another. Have you ever thought about harnessing this marvelous energy and making it work for you? Now, before you go off on a tangent or jump up and down or say, "Tension, marvelous? What are you, some kind of nut?" Let's talk about it, or rather, how about lending an ear (or an eye since you are reading) to what I have to say.

Now we all have anxieties, tensions, parental pressure and expectations that aren't always fulfilled. There are pressures of marriage, single life, alimony, ordinary run-of-the-mill daily pressures that make life so exciting and interesting. Sometimes we wonder if tension is necessary. In recent years, words like anxiety and tension have had negative connotations to such a degree, that more and more people are relying on tranquilizers and alcohol to rid themselves of tension-provoking thoughts and situations. The increase of alcohol and tranquilizer consumption is a matter of statistical record. (You can look up those records if you don't believe me.)

Relation of Tension to Awareness

Tension doesn't have to be eliminated entirely. I believe it can work positively for you. Tension acts as a signal to increase your awareness in a situation. When you let the tension control you, instead of the reverse, then you are not acting in your own best interests, that is, doing what is right for you. Tension tunes you in to something being not quite right or out of sync. Maybe the tension is just a slight discomfort over a decision you feel pressured into making. Without this awareness, you may not be able to think the situation through to a better conclusion. Tension is your intuition telling you to take time, to stop and think. Listen to it! Your body is trying to tell you something. You've got to start trusting yourself and your feelings sometimes and now is as good a time as any to begin.

The Relations of Tension to Motivation

By taking the time to think of whatever your tension is warning you about, you will be in a position to redirect it into new energy, energy that will give you the motivation you need to put your feelings into direct action.

Have you ever felt pressured at work or at home to complete a project that requires a longer period of time to get it done right? You try to do it quickly and get so tense, you really botch it up. Tension is warning you to Slow Down. For example, you decide to bake a last-minute cake before company arrives. You reason that it will be faster than running to the store to buy dessert. You mix up the old faithful, never-let-me-down recipe which doesn't rise and does let you down. Ultimately, you have to throw the whole mess down the garbage disposal because you forgot to add the baking powder. You wind up wasting more time and energy running to the store, maybe even getting a ticket on the way for being declared a local hazard and breaking speed records. To add insult to injury, as it were, you arrive back home breathless, sweaty and definitely uncool to find your guests wandering around the building, wondering if they were wrong about the date (The evening may have turned out okay eventually, but the tension made you a nervous wreck and kept you from enjoying life and your guests). When tension takes over and causes you to move in ways that defeat your purpose, use that energy and tension as motivation to accomplish the end goal in a more efficient way. Think of options other than the obvious one at the moment.

The Three R's

When important decisions are necessary and you feel pressured, challenge your tension with what I call the 3 R's. (W)rite, Read and Revise (Okay, so I am taking poetic license with the Write.) Take a piece of paper and make three columns with each word heading a column. Now, under "(W)rite," write down the tension provoking situation and the circumstances that produce or surround it. It doesn't have to be a whole megillah. A sentence or two will suffice. It will simply state what you think is the problem. Secondly, under the "Read" column, write down one word—"Solvable?" Now go back and read the problem you wrote down. If it doesn't seem to be solvable to you, if you are going around in circles with it, then to hell with it for now. This step in itself will eventually help you see things more clearly and feel less pressured. Get rid of the compulsion to find answers. Everything doesn't have an answer immediately. If you've shelved the compulsion to come up with a decision, you can avoid writer's cramp by waiting to see what goes under "Revise."

If the problem is solvable, if a solution is necessary, even earth-shattering, under "Revise," make a list of the possibilities and options you have for arriving at a solution to the problem. When you look at the options, you are in a position to select the best possible ways to solve the problem.

Now you are ready to take positive steps toward finding a solution. By now it may not even matter anymore. The problem may have disappeared as if by magic. Don't tackle too many problems at once. Better yet, take one at a time and eliminate the clutter. You aren't trying to win a bronze medal in the Olympics for problem-solving. Tackling one at a time will help you be more productive and effective (and less tense).

Since it is to your benefit to be able to turn the energy from tension into positive action, let's have a little rehearsal of one of the ways we can accomplish this not-so-easy feat. Try an exercise in Imagery at this time.

Close your eyes and imagine a *tense* situation, one in which you have to confront someone where your tension or anxiety level is high. (Are you feeling your stomach churn and throat dry? *That's tense!*) The situation might be asking your boss for a raise, dropping the idea of separate vacations to your mate, or something else you haven't had the guts to talk about before to that person—that same person who throws you for a loop. Once you begin to picture yourself in that tense scene, shift to a picture of yourself as being very calm while you are talking about the anxious situation. Don't chicken out now. Remember this is Imagery and you might as well practice getting over the anxiety. Now picture yourself saying to that person, "I'm really nervous about this"; and say it *out loud!* Talk to that person the way you wish you could, the way you've talked in your imagination, but never in person. Allow yourself to say what you've always wanted to say. After all, they really aren't around to make you feel uncomfortable. By voicing your feelings to yourself and eventually to the person or persons involved, you will relieve some of the tension and will be able to function in a more constructive and effective manner. With Imagery practice, you can reduce tension in anxious situations. Don't give up until you have the problem licked.

Use the mirror to practice, saying those things you wish you could say to another. Practice with friends, relatives, classmates *not* connected with the tense situation. Enlist their aid. Explain what you are doing and practice, getting the words down pat so that you won't have to fish for things to say when you do confront the problem.

Write out or tape the different ways you can approach the person involved. Force yourself to think of more than one or two ways. The more ways you think about, the better. Then you can choose the one you are most comfortable with. Plan what you will say. Don't trust to luck. This will help you gain better control of yourself and the situation.

Set up the space and environment you feel comfortable with when you are ready to tackle the situation. For example, if you can talk it out better over coffee, then set the time and place. Setting up a comfortable situation can even be done at work. If your employer paces behind a desk, looks out of the window, or uses other effective diversionary tactics, you can ask him or her to come and sit beside you. It's okay to say you would feel more at ease if. . . You can express your nervousness and say it is difficult for you to talk with the desk between you.

If you're out with a new date and the date appears preoccuppied while you are saying something important, you can ask your date to listen to you or express an opinion. Express your own discomfort over the situation without putting the other one down. It is important for you to be comfortable, especially when you are talking about something you haven't been able to discuss before.

You can initiate conversation in tense situations and clear the air by admitting you are tense. Having fear or anxiety doesn't make you a coward, it only means you have anxiety in this particular situation. The other person may even appreciate your honesty, and change attitudes and actions towards you. Remember, you have been conditioned to think that figures of authority, like employers, or people in positions of power are superior, and to treat them accordingly. Have you ever gone to a doctor's or lawyer's office with full intention of asking for information and didn't speak up because you had lost your nerve? You may have felt awed by their knowledge, their power or position which caused you to become tongue-tied. You may have even been angry at yourself upon leaving for not getting the information you wanted in the first place. This is an example of the kind of conditioning we've all had—not to challenge authority. Their knowledge and power doesn't make them superior. It only makes them more knowledgeable and expert in their field. Authority figures are human and have as many anxieties or hang-ups as the rest of us. Sometimes more.

Controlling Yourself

Say that you goof, get tongue-tied, screw up the conversation you planned so well, and you don't come across the way you would have liked. Say the boss decides you can't have that raise now, or an intimate relationship fizzles and everything goes wrong despite all your preparation and practice. Don't down yourself, don't waste time feeling guilty. Above all, don't overeat! These things don't solve anything. They only make you feel worse. Keep in mind it is only *one* goof, *one* mishandling of a situation, *one* disappointment—that's all and nothing more. Don't magnify it! Use the experience to learn how to work out future situations. Practice and improve your performance. Next time you'll know what to do. Let the tension work for you. Tell yourself one failure is not the end. It means you are trying to be more effective. Awareness of your weakness is a big step in controlling it. Say to yourself, "That's my weak spot, I have to work on what I'll say or do next time." Use skills like Imagery, to gain control of yourself.

Instead of backing off from a situation, think about what you would prefer to happen. Think and list options that might help you achieve your preferences. Realize that your anxiety is so real that it keeps you from acting. Whatever you do, don't add more tension by wondering *why* you feel so badly about blowing the situation, or wishing you were different (super smooth, cool, etc.) Now that you are face-to-face with the tension that controls you, practice convincing yourself that *you* can control *it*. If you allow the tension to take over and say nothing about a raise or change to your employer, if you expect the other person to read your mind ("They *should* know, haven't I hinted often enough?"), you will only wait around unhappy and unproductive because you don't get what you feel is your due. Prepare yourself. Act, don't Re-act!

The way to control the tension is to initiate a positive action in spite of the anxiety. Come on now, you can think of at least one. Stretch your imagination a little! You can broach the subject you want to talk about to your mate or your boss. If the other party tries to lay some guilt on you or makes you back down, you can say, "I wish I weren't so nervous about this, but I am. I need you to help me by listening to what I have to say." The more positively you act, the happier and less anxious you will feel in the actual confrontation. When your planning and strategy are ready and you are going to take the plunge and talk to that other person, select the action or actions you will take that arc most comfortable for you. Select those actions that work toward achieving what you want to achieve. The more you have planned, practiced and rehearsed, the more effective you will be and the better your chances are for achieving your goals. Don't forget to use the mirror to practice. The mirror is great for seeing yourself saying the words and the way in which you want to come across in the situation.

We are responsible for our own actions and working out problems as well as eliminating or reducing tension. We are responsible for our own growth. *You*, out there, are not just the result of strict parents, overbearing brothers and sisters, warped opinions and all the conditioning that you've blamed all these years for your own shortcomings. It is a damned shame you've learned to be weak in the knees when you stand up for your rights. Somewhere along the line you had to learn those responses. You can unlearn them and learn new ones that are not only more effective, but can make you feel a hell of a lot happier with yourself and stronger than you've ever felt in your life.

By practicing new responses, selecting things to say, listing other alternatives in communicating with others, and making your own active choices, you can modify your own behavior to suit your needs and wants. Practicing the new behavior helps to unlearn the anxiety-provoking responses you have already learned, responses you haven't been happy with. The standards of your past learned behavior were set by parents, society and whoever had a hand in controlling your actions and molding your character. You adopted those standards. They may have been necessary for your survival, but you are not that controlled little kid any more. History is an excuse. To say, "I can't help it, that's my nature," is avoiding the issue. To fall back on being a victim of conditioning is a cop-out.

Ask yourself a key question, "*How* can I help myself?" Then learn how to help yourself. Be boss of your own actions. Be selective. Look for ways to help yourself. You can be in control. It is up to you. Become increasingly aware of who you are by listing your own needs. Practice being up-front and expressing those needs. By increasing awareness of your own needs, what you really want, who you really are, you can then look at where you are headed and finally, what *you* have to do to get there. No one else has the power over you unless you give it to them.

If you've changed one small thing so far, accomplished some behavioral change that gave you a sense of self-esteem, confidence and energy you didn't have before, then you are beginning to glimpse the wonderful rewards in store that come with taking the responsibility of your own actions. You can do it. You can grow!

FOURTH WEEK ASSIGNMENT

Make a list of your needs. Select one particular relationship you have where those needs are not being fulfilled. How can you have those needs met? What can you do differently to accomplish what you'd like? Changing your pattern of behavior might be the growth the relationship needs—so—Let's Get Growing.

CHAPTER 5

EFFECTIVENESS

Achieving for Effectiveness

One positive thing that has gained nationwide recognition in recent years is the importance of physical fitness. Take care of your body. Regular exercise, even if it is only a few minutes daily, a balanced diet and plenty of rest will put you in a better frame of mind as well as give you more stamina. We need stamina to do the hundreds of things we do daily. Effective behavior needs energy behind it for thinking as well as doing. Start working on increasing your energy level.

If you are not motivated to exercise at home, find time to join a belly dancing class or something that will give your get-up-and-go a little pizzazz. Join an attractive neighbor or friend for a jog around the block in the early hours of the a.m. or evening. You might get a romance going, even if it is on the run. Being conscious of nutrition and eating energy foods will pay off as well as get your muscles in shape. Take care of the whole you. You will function better mentally, as well as physically. You can't think clearly or function well if you are dragging your aspirations. If you are prepared to function both physically and mentally, you can and will be more effective. (I know when I have had the proper amount of rest, exercise and high energy diet, I feel as if I can take on the whole world.) You owe it to yourself to feel the best you possibly can. After all, aren't you worth it?

Effectiveness through Planning

Once you make up your mind to feel and be effective, you have the power to be effective. To reach your goal, whether it is a raise, more power on the job, losing weight, overcoming shyness, having a more exciting sexual relationship, making friends—whatever you want to achieve, then it is necessary to have a plan. Zero in on the plan by writing down step-by-step how you are going to go about getting results. That will help you focus on the main issue, your goal. It will keep you from getting side-tracked. If it's weight you want to lose, don't set too high a standard for yourself. Set up a program you can follow realistically. Diet with a friend, join Weight Watchers or whatever feels right for you. Follow the plan if you really want results. If it's a dying romance you want to spark, try something new like taking a bubble bath together. Use your imagination. Don't wait around and keep putting off the action with excuses. Acting on the plan *quickly* will make you more effective and give you a sense of accomplishment. It will give the old self-esteem a shot in the arm. Make a commitment to your goal and work at it. The plan would include identifying *what* the problem is, *where* it happens, *how* it happens and *with whom* it exists. Refer to it often enough to increase your perception of the problem area and work toward the best ways to accomplish the end result. Focus on *how you can solve* the problem, not how overwhelming the problem itself is.

Be Prepared

If you have decided that your goal is to seek a position worthy of your newly discovered talents, then learn all you can about what that position requires. Take the time to get it all together, get more skill and information. When you are well prepared, you will achieve credibility by being knowledgeable, well informed and being in control. The information at your fingertips plus the way you present yourself are both important. When you know you look good, feel good and are prepared, you will come across the best way you can and you will feel good about yourself. (Another boost for your self-esteem.)

If you don't do well enough, if for some reason you don't get what you set out to get, that in itself can be a learning situation for the next time. This is your golden opportunity to grow some more by being honest with yourself. See if there is some way you can improve for next time. Write it down so you won't forget the successful components to be included in the next encounter. Remember, if your request is turned down, it is only one disappointment. The person who says "no" to your ideas may say "yes" the next time. Persistence sometimes pays off and you may want to raise the issue again when you feel the timing is right for you. Or perhaps simply more practice is needed.

Don't burn all your bridges by saying, "I'll quit/leave, etc. if you don't give me. . ." (not unless you really are going to leave). Let's say you've asked for a raise and your employer socks it to you with, "Well, if you're not happy here, you might try looking for another job." Before you let your anxiety push the panic button (assuming you didn't actually have leaving in mind), stay cool and say something like, "I really hadn't thought of leaving. I would like to stay with the company—I like it here.. What I would like to know is, if there is no possibility of a raise at this time, *when* can I expect one?" Get him or her involved in making some kind of commitment. Tell the employer why you think you deserve it and how you feel. (Don't say that you think he or she is a creep for not giving you what you want NOW!) If you don't get a commitment as quickly as you'd like, and think you might back down, hang in there by repeating, "When can we discuss a raise again, one month, two months?" Pin the evasive little devil down. Mark the date on your calendar. Ask your employer to mark the calendar for a future appointment and don't hesitate to remind the person of the commitment when it is due. Follow through.

In the meantime, think about alternatives to your approach next time and the preparation of a stronger strategy. If you use the time wisely, preparing for the replay, you will be cool and in control. You won't be fishing around for ideas and be caught off balance. Don't bicker, it will diminish your power and control of your actions. If things appear as if they are going to get our of hand, (if the other person is getting angry) instead of reacting to the anger, stay cool. You can do it. You've been practicing now for four chapters. Say calmly, "We can't function this way. I feel I'm not accomplishing what I came here for. I do want to discuss the possibility of. . .(whatever your goal is) and I need you to talk it over with me. Would you rather I come back another time?" Make sure you specify a definite return match, otherwise you'll be right back in anxiety land again. Give your arguments for your cause in a calm voice, even if it is difficult. *Act, don't React* when you are trying to accomplish a goal.

Be a person of your word, a person who is willing to be responsible for your share of the bargain. If you are the kind of person who threatens, "I'll leave" etc., idle threats that you use as a ploy, that doesn't do much for your credibility. Start being more realistic; be willing to work. If the boss says you have to improve before you can get a raise, ask to be shown exactly where those improvements are expected. Then at least you know which direction to take. When you become more expert at the job, better at handling a situation with a loved one, or make some change you hadn't been able to before, ask for more responsibility. Request more money, more authority, more sex—whatever realistically, you feel you deserve. If you are a person of your word, you will earn trust. Assuming responsibility for your own actions will build your confidence. It may also be frightening. Now is the time to realize, if you haven't already, you can't blame others for your problems. You stand or fall by yourself, on your own merit, by your own actions. If the thought is overpowering, try thinking about the power, the energy and the generally confident feelings that will accompany your being self-directed and in control. Think how great you will feel if you do get what you want.

"Okay," you might say, "I can do all these things, but how will I know if they work for me? Isn't my situation unique?" If you are looking for a written guarantee, one that covers a year's communication skills or a thousand hours of assertive technique warranty, whichever comes first, there is *no* guarantee. The only way to check out a situation and see if it works, is to try it. (The A-C-T method included.) All I am saying is, the skills do work. My students, my clients and I use them and discuss the results. The results are more confidence, more power and strength than we ever believed possible. If you practice your new behavior, you will increase the possibility of more workable situations and less anxiety. This is the only way to find out what works for you. Do it!

Practice using your inner strength. Don't be afraid to do the wrong thing. Fears, even imagined ones, have an extraordinary amount of control over what we do or don't do. Don't let them ruin this beautiful life of yours. Learn to accept yourself as one who will make mistakes. Life includes mistakes and hassle, accept it as such. Practice at least five minutes daily undoing some of the "musts". Ask yourself, "Must I *really* do this? Is this one of the 'shoulds' I've tried to live up to and felt uncomfortable with for so long?" Be open to change. Hanging on to the same old security blanket doesn't mean it's going to be there forever or keep you warm. Change, just for the sake of changing, can be fun and challenging. Change, with a goal toward growth and self-direction, can be a source of strength, no matter how many other changes occur in your lifetime. And those changes will occur.

Act *less* dependently on someone else and say to yourself, "I am on the way to making myself an autonomous person. I have the power to live my own life the way I choose. No one can have the power over me that I don't give them." Power is your ability to be effective, strong and sure of your own ability. You deserve to feel good about yourself. If you don't take this power for yourself, if you don't strive, you may wonder all your life what might have happened if only. . . We are living in an exciting age, doors are opening, but if you sit back and wait for someone to open them, you will only be a spectator in this wonderful game of life.

Don't make excuses for not acting, especially when it comes to your own best interests (things you want to achieve before you reach one hundred and say, "Why didn't I?") Accept *in*decision as part of your life. Weigh the advantages and disadvantages and look at the options in situations. If you are undecided, pick an alternative you think will be best for you, one you can live with and be comfortable with. Nobody says you have to make the right decision all the time, or any decision at all if you really don't want to. Don't punish yourself if you make a wrong decision occasionally. You are human and mistakes are allowed even if someone else doesn't think so.

Pay closer attention to how you handle situations, how you get your way, in personal situations that require more assertiveness than you usually show. For example, telling your mother-in-law you'd appreciate it if she'd listen to what you have to say instead of brushing you aside:" After all, we do love the same man, and we both are interested in his welfare, aren't we?" That's *one* way to get her to listen. Smile and don't use sarcasm. Once she gets over the shock of how pleasant you can really be, she may start reacting differently toward you. Both of you may even learn to respect and like one another.

Get in the habit of using Imagery to be more effective. Say the things over and over in your imagination that you wish you could say. See yourself performing effectively and keep repeating the image until you see yourself calm in the situation. The more you visualize yourself as calm and effective, the more likely you will come across that way.

Not acting or speaking up in a situation may be a way of inflicting self-punishment. You might be subconsciously (or consciously) telling yourself you don't deserve the good treatment from others or yourself. Maybe you feel you are not worthy of having it better this time around. The first step to feel worthy is to ACT positively and practice the skills you are learning as you read them in this book or learn them in my classes (or both). It may take a great deal of effort to get started. It may even be difficult at times, but start reaching out. When you do reach out, aim for the stars. Anything is possible.

FIFTH WEEK ASSIGNMENT

A. Start looking at yourself in new ways. Pay attention to your positive side. Go ahead, get used to seeing the good side of *You.*

B. Identify your assets by examining the things you do well. List them. Share them with other people and ask others what they think are your assets.

C. How did you feel when you told others? (Once the initial embarrassment and shock wore off.)

D. How did you feel when others gave their opinions? (Was it difficult to say "thank you" and accept a compliment?)

Note: Examining your assests can help you use them to make an experience more successful. The acceptance of your assets will also build your self-image. (You didn't think you had those assets, did you?) Learn to enjoy the positive things about yourself, you are okay. In class, we often discuss whether writing down assets and successes helps overcome the embarrassment of telling others about them. Most students feel that writing does reinforce the good self-image and makes it easier to share with others. They often preface their sharing with, "I'm somewhat embarrassed about this; this is new to me, but. . ." One of my students felt ill at ease saying something positive about himself. He usually began by making jokes or laughing nervously. He was finally able to get in touch with his own insecure feelings and share his assets. He even learned to ask for positive feedback. He said the positive feedback felt so good, he felt as if he were flying all day.

Now that you've started looking at your assets and successes, Grow On and be the somebody you always wanted to be.

CHAPTER 6

ASSERTIVENESS

By now, you may be pleasantly surprised to learn how good you can feel once you've changed those negative mental images to positive ones. Not only does the negative behavior change, but the emotions that follow begin to change also. You may not realize it as yet, but all that good energy and emotional good feeling is going to increase with each step you take (assuming you've been practicing diligently). Now you are going to learn Assertive Training in a way that will do you the most good, a practical way you can use successfully with the people you come in contact with. It is for you to use in your own interpersonal environment. You will be acquiring new verbal skills that will come in handy in uncomfortable situations when you feel put-down. Situations which cause you to act in self-defeating ways, that is, situations in which you don't say what you'd like to because of anxiety. Assertiveness will help you answer the put-down effectively right then and there, instead of wishing hours later you had thought of a comeback when you needed it.

Most books on Assertiveness start out full speed ahead in the first chapter to force-feed you, the reader, into being more assertive. Assertiveness, its concepts and practices, as you've noticed, is about the half-way point in the A-C-T Method. That did not come about by accident. It is my belief that we cannot make changes and adopt new ways (especially verbal skills) until we build awareness of the ways we already use. We have to know what to change as well as how to change it. The A-C-T Method is a crawl before you walk, practical approach. It doesn't work for everybody, but it has worked for hundreds who have tried it. It is easier to grow by stages. By common sense and reasoning how you got to where you are, you will reason how to get where you want to go. Let's grow into being more Assertive with a new awareness, one step at a time.

Even if you are aggressive, we are, as a whole, a passive people. We are afraid that if we express the way we really think, others won't like us. We've been taught that our inner feelings are often bad, so we learn to say the right thing—that is, whatever is acceptable to parents, teachers, church—society in general. We've been taught to conform and stay in line. Let's face it, that makes it easier for authority to control us. (Control is often necessary in society.) We learn to smile and hide our anger. We also learn to cover up our frustrations. When somebody steps on our toes or runs over us in the supermarket, we learn to smile despite the pain. We say "Don't worry about it, think nothing of it," when what we'd really like to do is punch them in the nose. That kind of learned suppression and the frustration that accompanies it is baloney. It only leads to misery. It's not necessary to feel frustrated and carry it around inside until you explode at the kids or someone else you love. Neither is it necessary to punch someone in the nose. You can learn to speak up tactfully without fear and with less anxiety. That's what Assertiveness is all about—improving communication skills while reducing anxiety. Being honestly Assertive is good for you and the people around you. The intent of Assertive Behavior is to communicate honestly and directly with consideration of your feelings and the feelings of others, whether it is in a social, business or sexual context. Learning how to speak up, learning how to say yes or no, when *you* want to, not because you think you should, is Assertive.

Basic Concepts

Before the program gets into the various styles and their differences (Aggressive, Passive, Assertive; remember, this is a step-by-step, crawl before you walk method), I'd like to share with you some of the concepts of Assertive Behavior so you will have some guidelines to follow as you learn how to be more Assertive.

Lack of Assertive Behavior has received increasing attention as a clinical problem in recent years. There are many definitions of Assertiveness. Approaches to training are varied. However, certain facets of Assertiveness have been agreed upon by leading psychologists and teachers. Those definitions are as follows: (a) Standing up for one's rights; (b) Refusing to comply with seemingly unreasonable demands (author's note—if the demand puts pressure on you and causes a great deal of anxiety, I consider that a seemingly unreasonable demand); (c) Making requests and reasonable demands of others (author's note—without resorting to manipulation and disregard for another) and; (d) Generally, overtly expressing both positive and negative feelings to others (author's note—*how* those feelings are expressed is important—Grow on!).

*Un*assertive people have difficulty meeting their social, sexual and material needs because they do not speak up. They are afraid if they say what they want to, they run the risk of disapproval or rejection. As a consequence, *un*assertive people are often exploited, pushed aside or ignored in the bustle of everyday living. Rather than take an active part in decision-making, problem-solving or directing their own lives, *un*assertive people are acted upon.

Who needs it? You may not believe this, but we all need assertive training. All of us would like to have some counter-influence on our interpersonal environment at some time, especially when we ordinarily feel helpless, powerless or frustrated. We need it at those particular times when our needs are not being met. We all need to know how to handle those instances when we *re*act rather than act; those same instances that are not only self-defeating, but often leave the other party upset, confused and angry at us.

We need to communicate and share warm feelings with the people who cross our paths. For example, let's say a loved one blames you for something and you feel hurt, or you feel the accusation is unfair. You don't speak up for fear you will make things worse by getting involved in an argument. What happens? You get choked up, give in, don't make waves and then hate yourself for not saying anything. Here is a need for Assertiveness. You might even be told by your employer that your work hasn't been up to par and you'd better shape up or ship out. Even though you may be sure you are not at fault, you find yourself choking up and remaining silent rather than risk a direct confrontation with the boss. Another case for Assertiveness. Taking control of your own actions doesn't necessarily mean you have to be aggressive or domineering. Taking control of your actions and speaking up does mean learning to handle situations to the best of your new Assertive Ability—the kind of handling that makes you feel good about yourself and others. Both you and others involved might gain a whole new respect for *you*.

Some of us may be Assertive in handling business problems and not personal problems, or vice versa. However the case, we all need it sometime, somewhere. Happiness is having Assertive-nsss at your fingertips when you need it!

Learned Behavior

Assertiveness is a skill you can learn. You may already have learned some Assertiveness in your childhood, certainly in cases where your parents had definite expectations about your behavior. For example, if you are male, you were encouraged in "manly ways" (fight back, don't be a sissy, etc.). Those same behaviors may have been discouraged if you are female. This kind of cultural stereotyping—the "passive, nice little girl" and "the aggressive male," are not the only ways to communicate. Society perpetuates similar images and roles throughout our lives.

In business if a man is pushy, he is referred to as aggressive with respect for his shrewdness and his ability to get ahead. The same behavior in a woman is often labeled as a castrating female, opinionated bitch, ball-crusher, etc. Her loss of femininity is often implied and generally the labels applied to her are put-downs. A woman can be both feminine and professional. Being aggressive or competitive in business doesen't make her less a female. Fear of being judged overbearing, pushy, castrating or even lesbian has traditionally kept women *un*assertive in our society. The individual, whether male or female, has the right to choose actively a passive, aggressive or assertive way to communicate and act, without sexual implication.

In addition to the role models provided by assertive parents or teachers, other influences on whether or not we exhibit Assertive Behavior might be similar displays of assertiveness among our peers. The important thing to remember is that assertiveness, or lack of it, is learned. Because you haven't learned to be assertive up to this point, don't give up and say, "That's the way I am." Since you had to learn to be *un*assertive, you can learn to be assertive. If you've been practicing the skills so far, you are already on your way. There are probably lots of things you never thought you could do until you tried. Try being assertive. You will begin to feel more confidence than you believed possible.

Assertive Programming

One of the main objectives of this program is to motivate behavioral change from passive and aggressive to assertive styles. You will be learning techniques as you read (and practice) that can help form the foundation of Assertive Behavior. The techniques and skills involved are for you to use and be what you want to be. Get in the habit of using them.

In developing Assertive Behavioral skills, it is essential to practice situations where assertiveness is needed. This kind of practice will help you know what to do or say at the time you need to do or say it. The practice will also increase your awareness so that you can quickly pick up on when to use appropriate responses or lead the way in a sticky situation. Appropriate responses, in this case, do not mean what you think the other person might like to hear, but rather, the kind of responses which permit you to be in control of your own thoughts and words. Those appropriate responses will prevent you from being manipulated and can be used to effectively work out negotiations or compromises you feel comfortable with. It is important to remember that the Assertive Style respects others as well as yourself. It demonstrates how developing communication skills can help you control your own behavior, direct your own life and develop confidence.

"I" is the Key

The key to more Assertive Behavior is the use of *I*. "I am in control. *I* can act." Awareness of when you are passive or or aggressive is the first step in acquiring assertive verbal habits. You will learn how to say "no" without a put-down and how to respond to someone who puts you down. The Assertive way is to make a statement beginning with "I," not "you." "I feel unhappy, frustrated, etc., when you don't give me an answer," not, "Why aren't you answering me, why do *you* do this to *me*?" The use of the I Factor will eliminate getting trapped into arguments that go around in circles. It is focusing on your feelings and then saying "I prefer," or "I want," etc., rather than blaming another. Accusations only lead to unsatisfying communication for both. If another person habitually puts you down and you decide to speak up about it (after more practice), instead of saying something like "Don't do that," and putting them on the defensive, you can say, "I am bothered by that and I would appreciate not hearing that again." Assertiveness deals with *how* verbal skills are used. Saying "I'd appreciate," or "I want," are only two ways to use it.

Behavioral Styles

So far, I have talked about Assertive Training in general; now let's be more specific and get down to the basic styles in order to recognize the differences with which you will be working. Behavior can't be reinforced effectively unless it has a solid foundation. (You are going to be so strong, you won't believe yourself!) To retrace steps a moment, I mentioned awareness of passive, aggressive and assertive behavior as the first step in being in control. What is meant by Passive, Aggressive or Assertive Styles of behavior? The following definitions will clarify the various styles for you to facilitate your own Assertiveness.

The Passive Style

If I could sum up this style in just two words, they would be "avoids conflict." The passive person usually is taken advantage of and usually has his/her rights violated. It isn't usually difficult to recognize the person who doesn't want to make waves and chooses peace at any price. This is the type who says, in a whiny voice, "I don't mind" (but really does) and gives in, even though the gut feeling knows it's wrong. Often, this type gives in and suffers headaches, ulcers, etc. The passive person is one who often acts the part of the supermartyr and becomes the victim of the aggressor.

Conditioning we learned as tots, feelings we learned to suppress, e.g., that it's not nice to swear or shout, are carried over into adult life. The passive style reflects the carryover and influences individuals, so that they do not do what they really want. Passive behavior often results in a great deal of tension for the individual. This kind of suppression erases the "self." It is letting someone else tell you how you should live, defining your role in life for you. You are not making active choices for yourself. No wonder the passive person feels uncomfortable. Passive people often feel frustrated, unhappy, hurt, anxious, exploited, rejected and do not usually achieve their goals. They give in saying "yes" when they want to say "no." In sexual relationships, they say "no" when they really want to say "yes." They often blame others for putting the pressure on them, knowing full well they will weaken. If one *allows* manipulation, another person is not to blame. To feel used, abused, or manipulated, Mr. or Ms. Passive has to *allow* it.

If you recognize yourself as being passive, learn not to allow manipulation by eliminating some of the pressure on yourself. It's okay to tell the other person you can't handle it, or would prefer not to, when the pressure is on. You are entitled to say "no" to a request if you like, without inventing excuses. It won't be easy, but you will like yourself a whole lot more. You may eventually rid yourself of tension, headaches and household pests who put the squeeze on you. Chances are these household pests tell you how great you are for doing all you do, then tell others what a patsy you really are. It's all right to do favors for people, but not at the expense of a great deal of pressure and anxiety for yourself. Start being good to *you!*

The Aggressive Style

This is the style that is out to dominate, to get one's way at the expense of others. This often totally erases the other person. Whether you come on like gangbusters or deny being aggressive and manipulate subtly—either way, you are still using manipulation to win at any price (if you are not aggressive, don't skip over to the next style; after all, you do need to know how to deal with aggressive people and learn to recognize their tactics, if you haven't already). The price of winning might very well be the loss of friendship, loss of a mate, loss of business deals, even physical symptoms like migraines, high blood pressure and heart attacks. The price of winning is often too high. An aggressive person may achieve goals, but is most often explosive, angry and overbearing. Aggressive people are usually insecure and defensive. Because they are often defensive, they humiliate others, intrude on other people's choices and act in an overbearing manner intended to put the other guy down. This tactic supposedly gives their own egos a boost. Many admitted aggressors (in my classes), have told me they didn't have a good opinion of themselves after aggressive outbursts. Most agreed that guilt often accompanied these outbursts. With aggressive communication, when control is lost, often the content or main issue gets lost also. Aggressive interactions that are characterized by caustic remarks, more than likely will offend and alienate other people. The person who is great at dishing it out and unable to take it, is more than likely a member of this category. Assertiveness would be most beneficial here in learning to win friends and influence people in a less pushy manner.

The Assertive Style

Many people confuse assertiveness with aggression. Nothing could be further from the truth. The Assertive Style differs from the Aggressive Style in the manner in which it is delivered. Assertive expressions are usually positive statements made in tactful ways (the aggressive person is not the epitome of tact). Being assertive doesn't involve hurting or putting down another individual. The assertive person focuses on achieving goals without hurting others, feels good about "self," has confidence and self-esteem. The assertive person is emotionally, socially and sexually expressive, makes her/his own choices and acts in his/her own best interests without undue anxiety. Assertive people focus on outward expression, not on harboring resentments or building anxieties until the "lid" blows off, a situation that leaves other persons wondering what the hell that was all about.

Being assertive is knowing that you can't usually solve anything yelling. Bickering diminishes your power and ability to control yourself. Assertive people practice keeping cool and know it isn't always easy to do. It's okay to be angry, but it's *how* you handle it that counts. (More about this later.) If you slip and lose your cool, you are not a failure. Keep trying. The more you practice, the easier it gets.

As an example of an assertive exchange, let's say you hired someone to repair your dishwasher and the result was unsatisfactory. You call the repairman again and get nowhere. Instead of being frustrated with him for giving you the run-around, before you decide to pay someone else to do it over, handle it assertively. For example, ask him to come back and repair it correctly (not just to look at it). If he refuses, repeat that you want it done (no matter how busy he says he is). Pin him down to a definite date. Tell him you expect the job satisfactorily completed (to your satisfaction). Don't get sidetracked into an argument. If he tells you that you are too fussy, etc., tell him that was why you selected his shop—you had heard it was a reliable company with outstanding help. Concentrate on getting the job done. Write a letter to the boss of the company if you have to. Without the put-down, express your inconvenience, how you feel (and surely the waste of company time), the necessity of writing, waiting for the repairman, etc. It is okay (and assertive) to include an extra jolt if the job is not done to your satisfaction. Say (or write), "I hope it won't be necessary to go to my attorney or Consumers' Affairs about this." Keep a carbon copy of your letter and follow it through by a call back several days later. That way they can't ignore you.

You don't have to apologize for what is your due. It isn't necessary to say "I'm sorry to have bothered you." You are the one who is bothered in the situation. *(They owe you* an apology for not doing it right the first time.) You don't have to be overbearing or pushy. Stay cool and even-tempered and focus on the main issue. Get the job done! Be Assertive!

You will be learning from here on in, many skills and techniques designed to help you to be more assertive and reduce your anxiety level in situations that bother you. The skills will be valuable in social situations, meeting new people and other unfamiliar or familiar situations that may be highly anxious for you. Social assertiveness can be beneficial in making new friends while at the same time, reducing your anxiety. You don't have to be the life of the party, neither do you have to be on the outside looking in and wishing you could be less lonely. The skills can help you increase your pleasure while being a part of the social scene. You can use the skills to be more comfortable (and more assertive) in dating as well as mating.

SIXTH WEEK ASSIGNMENTS

A. Write a situation down that you "normally" handle unsatisfactorily. Now write down how you could handle (or wish you could handle) the same situation. Discuss what you think would be the "successful" experience with an interested party. Help him/her to become interested by talking about what you are learning and enlisting their help. Ask her/him to share how she/he handles a similar situation. Concentrate on what specific things (words, body language, tone of voice, etc.) make it successful.

B. Practice those successful assertive components that you've discovered.

C. Identify Assertive Behavior in other people and analyze what makes it 'Assertive' in your opinion. Build your awareness. Now Grow On to skill learning.

CHAPTER 7

SOCIAL SKILLS

Situational Social Skills

Many individuals experience difficulty and discomfort in social interaction with others. You may not be able to converse comfortably because you lack verbal skills. Perhaps you lack ability to handle situations where there are conflicting differences of opinion. You might be embarrassed, shy or reticent about expressing positive feelings, either giving a compliment or receiving one. It may even be difficult for you to express love or approval. Perhaps you experience discomfort when you are physically close to or touch people you know only casually. Situations in which discomfort and anxiety exist are many and varied.

Our society has discouraged comfortable feelings in many situations. For example, we have not been encouraged to reach out physically and touch others. Hugging someone of your own sex often carries sexual connotations. Consequently, we hold back instead of expressing closeness. In Latin countries it is the norm for men to embrace one another. The same behavior in our society is treated with frowns, raised eyebrows and labels of "gay," "fag," etc. By holding back, we miss out on many close, warm experiences. When the occasion presents itself to reach out and touch someone, we control the urge to hug, often feeling ill at ease. We have all felt these discomforts at one time or another. Have you ever stopped yourself from touching someone because you thought it was wrong? Permit yourself to shake hands, touch someone on the arm, hug, etc., in communication. Others may be surprised at your demonstrative display and pull away at first, only because they are not used to it. Once people get used to the idea, they usually enjoy it a great deal.

In class, we engage in an exercise at this point in which we reach out and touch the people next to us. Once the initial embarrassment passes, people really become involved in the exercise by invariably getting up from their seats, walking around the room and hugging everybody in class (without prompting from me). Then we discuss the initial reactions and the subsequent reactions once the embarrassment or discomfort has disappeared. As a rule, people smile more and loosen up. They discuss what a warm experience it was, sharing closeness with people they had never shared with before. The touching exercise adds a new and delightful dimension to the class. It stimulates conversation, sharing and open discussion of hang-ups, conditioning and inhibitions. It also brings about new awareness of our own feelings and the feelings of others who would ordinarily be the ships we pass somewhere in the night.

Many of the discomforts we experience in social encounters are due to the lack of appropriate social skills. We may have learned to be socially skillful with the "correct" behavior we should exhibit in public, for example, "Don't eat with your mouth open," or "Don't cause a scene." For the most part, we have not been conditioned to display warmth to strangers or to communicate honestly. We have not been taught how to meet new people or establish relationships. If we had learned social communication skills and felt at ease using them, we wouldn't be uncomfortable in social situations. The deficits that prevent us from interacting with others might only be restricted to a few situations. For example, a business executive might be socially adept with his or her peers, but may have difficulty communicating with family members and friends. There may be certain people in your life you have difficulty with, but not with others. Communication patterns are learned. You can learn new patterns to apply to your own specific difficult situations.

An extremely difficult social situation is one in which the single person, either widowed or divorced, finds the need to begin dating again and experiences the discomfort of not knowing where or how to begin. Many of the singles who attend my lectures have told me how anxiety prevents them from interacting. The anxieties are compounded by loneliness and depression when they do try to go out socially. Their pain is real. The fear of rejection is real (I know, I have been there.)

Several studies have been made on depression with striking evidence that "depressed people make fewer positive statements and communicate with fewer people than do non-depressed people" (Libet and Lewinsohn, 1975). Other studies (McLean, Ogston and Grauer, 1973) have shown that increased social interaction has been associated with reduction in depression. In other words, the more you interact, the more you learn and develop the habit of making positive statements to others, the more likely you will reduce depression. You may eliminate the depression altogether. Making *positive* statements to others, therefore, is an important step in developing your social skills and reducing depression.

Techniques for developing your social skills have to be rehearsed and practiced until they fit like a second skin. The first uncomfortable skin is the one that needs shedding. Let's say you are living alone, perhaps divorced or widowed. You decide to force yourself to go to some social gathering and meet someone of the opposite sex who looks interesting to you. Because you are female and may have been taught to be passive, you wait for him to approach you. You don't make a move. Anxiety may inhibit or paralyze you to such a degree that you don't even have conversation with him. He will never know you wanted to meet him. Sometimes your reticence or shyness is mistaken for aloofness or a non-caring attitude and you miss an opportunity for what may be interesting conversation, a new sex partner or. . .?

Before you do meet someone, before your next social encounter, let's rehearse some new behavior patterns to get you growing. Look at yourself in the mirror (concentrate on the words for now, not the new wrinkles). Repeat: "The next time I want to meet someone I want to talk to, I *can* ignore my anxiety, it won't kill me. I *can* walk up to him (or her) and say, "Hi, my name is. . .and I would like to meet you."

Try it, it is only unsettling at first. Get used to it. The discomfort will disappear. Keep the goal in mind, that is, meeting people. If you overhear some conversation that seems interesting, regarding a recent book or lecture, for example, so much the better. You can say, "I heard you talking about. . . and I'd like to know more about it. Can you tell me?" (Remember the open-ended question?)

Find out what others like, *their* interests and feelings about the subject. Share your feelings. If the conversation proves interesting, if a person turns out to be someone you may want to know better, initiate the relationship and suggest talking further over coffee or. . .? Suggest visiting an art show, places of mutual interest (or new interests). Exchange phone numbers, availability, etc.

If you write down and rehearse beforehand some sample questions or lines of patter and commit them indelibly to your memory (Practice, Practice!), you won't have to grope for words when the time comes. You won't have to add embarrass-

58

ment at being tongue-tied to your already conditioned anxiety. You can't anticipate conversation, but you can practice key phrases.

If the other person isn't as responsive as you'd like, don't withdraw. Don't magnify their behavior into a huge rejection. They may be lacking Assertive Skills and be as anxious as yourself in new situations. Concentrate on what *you* are going to do to get over the discomfort, the loneliness and depression. Don't let the fear of possible rejection prevent you from acting and enjoying your life.

Simple Skills to Practice

(1) *Act independently of your feelings.* Now before you jump all over me, accuse me of flipping out for sure this time, or tell me that feeling one way and acting another is phony (I've been accused of that by experts), let me elaborate and clarify what is meant by this basic skill.

Now most of us feel anxious in new situations. In order to get over anxiety, sometimes we force ourselves to act in ways we wouldn't ordinarily consider. We might *force* ourselves to approach a stranger at a party. Forcing yourself to act is one example of acting independently of feelings. The purpose of acting dependently of your feelings in anxious situations, is to use those techniques you've been practicing and concentrate on overt behavior (things you say and do), rather than on what you are wishing you could do (covert).

Compare "acting independently" with a responsibility you may already have assumed many times in your life. For example, you get up some mornings with the feeling that you'd rather spend the day at the beach than go to work. You really drag yourself around getting ready, poking around, deciding what to wear, plucking a practically invisible hair, etc. Once you down the second cup of coffee, put on your make-up (or shave), put a little pressure on yourself and get to work, you still feel as though you'd rather be at the beach. However, work is not quite the drag you thought it would be. In fact, once at work and engaged in conversation, you can make plans with someone to go to the beach over the weekend. You can suggest the idea to that cute co-worker you've been eyeing for some time. Once you're at work, it may not be the greatest day you've ever had, but it turned out okay. You acted independently of your feelings.

You don't have to make a big production of the acting, not unless, that is, you work in a TV or recording studio, or a talent agency and want to land a contract or make a big impression. As you gain experience, you will elaborate on your communication skills. The elaboration will build as you acquire confidence.

(2) *Modeling.* Observe someone who is successful in a similar social or business situation (if you observe people in a similar sexual situation, you can use modeling there also). It isn't necessary to envy the model and remain silent or inactive, wishing you could be the social (or sexual) butterfly. Use that person as a model and perform similar, successful behavior. You don't have to use the exact language and mannerisms, but try them on for size. Eventually you will find your own way and use what you feel comfortable with. By observing and using the model's skills, you will be learning additional effective behavior to get the desired results. You can use these behaviors in the kind of interaction you wish to engage in. Modeling is an effective clinical technique used by leading therapists.

In class we often set up situations between two people to demonstrate the use of Modeling. One is asked to be the employer and the other, the employee. The employee is supposed to ask for a long overdue raise and be extremely anxious about approaching the employer. The employer is instructed to be evasive and manipulative. There is no written script. The models play it by ear, each trying to win his/her point. After the performance, there is a lively discussion concerning the effectiveness of both employer and employee. How was the tone of voice, eye contact, posture, content and fluency of the conversation? Was the employee assertive? What particular things could the employee use to improve effectiveness and get that promised raise without causing a scene? How could the employee handle the anxiety?

A sample dialogue to make the employee more effective in this situation might be as follows:

Employer: I can't promise a raise right now, things are bad, business is off. If you feel you can better yourself somewhere else—well, that's up to you."

The employee may feel obligated to quit in this situation. However, rather than make a drastic move, here was an assertive communication that was suggested.

Employee: I really hadn't thought of leaving. Since I like my job, I would prefer to stay with the company. What I would like to know is, if I can't get the raise now, when do you think I could expect one?" or "How can I upgrade my work or qualify for a raise in the near future? Pin down the "when" exactly: e.g., next Thursday, the first of the month.

Clearly the task here is to get to the point quickly and eliminate the passive "Why can't I get my raise?" You'll be snowed by the number of reasons why you can't. Focus on getting a commitment, a deadline and follow through with, "You mentioned we would talk about a raise today, When can I expect it?"

Many times we have several sets of models perform a similar scene so we can compare performances and see the most successful components. Particular attention is paid to everything from confident body language (steady gaze, even controlled voice, etc.) to choice of words. Build awareness by observation. Build confidence by using Modeling.

(3) *Imagery.* Another technique to develop your social skills is Imagery. Imagine yourself in a social situation you "normally" don't handle well. Maybe you are uptight asking for a date or sit in a corner somewhere by yourself rather than take part in a social conversation. It's not because you don't want to be a part of it, it's because the knots in your stomach and the perspiration dripping down your back are too real and prevent action. You may even be embarrassed about asking your host or hostess where the bathroom is until you are very uncomfortable, and you preface your questions with an apology. For example, "Excuse me," or "I'm sorry to bother you, but. . ." It isn't necessary to apologize for getting what you want.

If you practice Imagery, thinking about and picturing yourself as more assertive (calm voice, positive action, etc.), you will be better prepared to speak up. Say, "Where is the bathroom? Can I please have. . .? No, thank you, I'd prefer not to. . ." without apology. By picturing yourself the way you would like to perform, down to the smallest detail (time, place, what you're wearing, *how* you are speaking, etc.), you increase the likelihood of performing the way you secretly want to. Imagery is another effective tool used by psychologists. Work on it!

(4) *Role-Playing.* You can practice and rehearse your desired

behavior, that is, the way you want to act with friends or family. It is usually better to practice in the classroom or with a group working out similar situations. Family and friends may not be receptive. You can explain, without apology, that you are attempting to work on a problem area. Share with them how modeling and Imagery help you to know *what* to practice. Ask for suggestions if you feel you can handle them. The suggestions may not be what you'd like to hear.

Ask for help. It is okay to say, "I need all the help I can get." You may run the risk of being turned down or ridiculed; however, don't allow others to deter you from your goal of growing and being more effective. Others may try to put you down because they are insecure and can't handle growth in you. If that does happen, learn to speak up without being defensive. You can say, "You may think it's dumb (if they say that), however, I'm finding that practice is helpful in overcoming anxiety. You might be interested in Assertive Training for yourself sometime." Leave it at that. You might like to ask your helper to point out your strong points and get some feedback on those. If they insist on pointing out your weaknesses, ask them to stick to the strengths at this time.

Maximize the Positive

Assertive Training has been focusing on helping you express yourself in a more effective way socially. With only one of the practices mentioned so far as a point of departure, you can within minutes unlock a vast treasury of colorful, exciting ways to be part of the social scene. By changing ineffective behavior to effective behavior, you can stimulate awareness, sharpen your communication skills and add punch to your life. Since it is important to know how to maximize the positive effects you have on others, then it follows that aggressive behavior would be counter-productive in the long run.

Sometimes anxiety causes people to act aggressively. Does this happen to you? Do you react aggressively in situations and then get angry at yourself for getting angry? You are not alone. This is a common occurrence. You can see (and experience) that *re*actions such as losing your temper and getting mad at yourself don't help you overcome the initial anxiety. Whenever you find yourself in a situation that evokes an aggressive reaction from you, practice keeping cool. (See simple skills 1.)

Then you won't have to compound the anger with guilt. It is time to change that unrewarding patter of behavior. It will take practice to change it. *Act, don't React!*

List the things you could say beforehand so you won't get trapped into the same old patterns. Maximize your positive actions and feelings by sharing them with the object of your anger. "I'd rather not get into an argument about it," "I do want to make this point," "We can't accomplish anything fighting about it," etc. Focus on *what* it is you want to accomplish. Tell the other person how good you feel being able to control your reaction and not get angry as you used to. Share your positive responses and feelings. Develop the habit of maximizing the positives in your life and minimizing the negatives.

Expressing positive feelings helps you minimize anxiety. You may never entirely rid yourself of anxiety, frustrations, or inhibitions in social (or sexual) intercourse, but by maximizing positive action, you will minimize the negative actions that ordinarily cramp your style and prevent you from having rewarding relationships. To gain the social skills mentioned earlier, systematic learning is important. Make a list of a few things you will try. Try them out in your next social encounter. If they don't work for you, add to or subtract from your list until you have a combination of skills and techniques that do. You can choose a combination that makes you comfortable, effective, and gets others to interact with you.

No one system is right for everybody. If you acquire, practice and rehearse elements of those skills, you will find what is right for you. You will find them invaluable, especially in situations where you wished you had spoken up or said something else. It will take some experimenting. Enjoy the discovery of experimenting. Don't down yourself for not being perfect. You will develop your own unique style that meets your particular needs. You don't have to change the whole you. You don't have to be pushy. You can't change unrewarding behavior by just reading and listening. You have to ACT! Accept the responsibility for making your life more fulfilling.

You are responsible. We often find ourselves in the uncomfortable position of facing anger, our own as well as someone else's. An important step in non-destructive expressions of anger, hostility or resentment is to remember, when you feel angry, it doesn't make the other person stupid. You are the one

63

who is feeling the anger. Accept the responsibility of your own feelings without blaming another person. They didn't *make* you mad. What they may have done was touch a sore spot, but that sore spot is strictly yours. Your feelings are part of you and tell you whether or not you are in rhythm with yourself. Your feelings, even angry ones (danger signals), are important data. Acknowledging and expressing your feelings is part of being assertive. Remember it's *how* you express them that counts. Get your message across without alienating the other person.

If you are so angry or hostile that you feel you are going to lose control, you can use physical expressions to relieve the tension. Stomp around or let out a roar if you have to. Don't use the put-down or blame. If you find you have to leave the room to cool off, tell the other person you need to cool off and will be back in a few minutes. Focus on communicating your discomfort and what you will do. Don't focus on the anger. Say that you are angry, or you need to remove yourself, for example.

Sometimes we overreact to a situation. Maybe we suppressed anger in the past because of our conditioning. Certain feelings, especially intensely emotional outbursts, have been X-rated in our society. Expressing anger is considered a no-no. Anger is often suppressed by both sexes to gain approval or acceptance. The suppression of anger often backs up and builds pressure, with the result that we blow up over some trivial thing, often days after the incident. Often, the blow-up had nothing to do with what caused the hostility in the first place. The other party involved is often stunned at your overreaction. You may experience mixed feelings of discomfort and amazement that you were so touchy. If you find you are ready to explode, there are ways to handle it that are socially acceptable as well as able to relieve your own tension.

Some effective assertive verbal expressions you might try on for size when you are angry are:

"*I* am (very) angry. . .," *not* "You make me angry."

"*I* strongly disagree," *not* "Why are you so opinionated?"

"*I* am extremely upset (or disturbed) by what you said," *not* "You said a dumb thing."

"*I* really don't like that and don't care to hear it again."

"*I* would prefer if you talk to me instead of shouting."

You get the idea? Deal with *I*—your personal feelings. You

will come up with many effective verbal (and assertive) expressions of your own if you take the time to think about them before the angry situation occurs. Memorize effective verbal expressions so that they will be part of your natural behavior.

Swear if you have to. You can say "Damn it, I am mad and I'm going to walk away for a few minutes, but I'll be back as soon as I simmer down." These are good devices for releasing strong feelings without aggression toward another person. Practice avoiding sarcasm and the put-down. Aggressive comments usually are caustic remarks that incense the other party, add to the argument and may result in alienation and isolation. You don't have to feel guilty for feeling anger. You have all kinds of feelings. What you are trying to accomplish is a way of coping with anger effectively. Effective coping with problem situations will be possible by keeping cool, keeping positive and keeping focused on main issues, as well as expressing your feelings.

SEVENTH WEEK ASSIGNMENT

A. Write out ways to express anger and annoyance without being insulting, accusing or aggressive. Memorize and practice several ways. After each expression, how do you feel? Which ones do you feel comfortable with?

B. List five situations that "make" you angry.

C. How do you handle them? How would you like to handle them? Rehearse ways you could handle them.

D. If you decide to handle an angry situation this week, select the one out of the five on your list that has the least potential for boiling over. Build your assertive skills by degrees, starting with the lowest risk situation. Build your self-esteem and confidence as you grow.

Now Grow On and acquire more coping skills.

CHAPTER 8

COPING SKILLS

Nowhere is skill more needed than in relating to others. We need all the help we can get in order to communicate effectively and tackle problems. Our education has neglected the social and sexual skills we need to get along with other people, often with those we most want to get along with. Knowing how is a matter of learning and applying particular techniques to the situations that arise. When we apply the know-how, when we communicate our feelings and accomplish what we set out to do, we feel good about ourselves. Good feelings follow positive action. When someone criticizes us or puts us down, if we handle the situation assertively, we feel damn good about ourselves. Feeling good is what Let's Get Growing (the A-C-T Program) is all about. By learning new skills that increase your strengths, you will like yourself more than you dreamed possible.

Skills need not be complicated. As a matter of fact, they need to be simple, easy to use and ready at a moment's notice when you need them. You will have them ready if you practice daily. The skills will be natural behavior, ready to help you handle the put-down, the aggressive individual, the elusive employer, the social and sexual relationships you want to improve your life. They (the skills) won't get you everything you want, but they will help you work more effectively in your attempts to achieve your goals.

There are many skills and techniques in addition to the ones mentioned so far. Additional coping skills that are easy to use and very effective are ones we try on for size by role-playing them in class. Some are borrowed from the book "When I Say No I Feel Guilty" (see References). For our purpose, they are listed in the order we learn them in the classroom situation.

Coping Skills

A. *Broken Record.* This is just what it appears to be, the persistent repetition of a phrase or sentence. Use the Broken Record to communicate what you want, need, feel, etc., *no matter how the other party tries to sidetrack or manipulate you.* Use the Broken Record technique to get your point across. Keep calm. If the other person says, "Why are you saying no? You've always said yes before. You've changed." Persist and repeat, "I do have to say no at this time." Don't worry about repeating it often. That is what makes the Broken Record effective. By constant repetition, sticking to a simple and short sentence or two, the other party will eventually get the point and stop. If they don't stop, if they try to bully you, if you feel yourself weakening, repeat your statement and say you have to leave. It's okay to say you don't like feeling pressured. Use repeated, persistent communication, like the Broken Record, so that you can remain in control. It will prevent you from getting hooked into a situation that is not right for you.

B. *Fogging.* This is one of my favorites. If someone criticizes you and you are at a loss, Fogging is a great way to handle it. Fogging is agreeing with the truth, agreeing with the principle or criticism levelled at you and expressing your own opinion to say you aren't buying the remarks. For example, someone says, "You're getting a little paunch there, aren't you, fatso?" Don't waste time feeling crushed. Use fogging in this way: "That may be true, *BUT* I really don't want to hear about it." If the other person persists in the put-down, repeat the message (Broken Record) and add that you do not want to hear it *again*. Period! Agreeing with critics (that you are heavier) often disarms them. They are not usually ready to have you agree. They are often only prepared to put you down and thereby make themselves feel more important. They might even have the attitude of "misery loves company" that is, "I'm not the only one getting fat."

C. *Your Track Record.* This is a way of being systematic. Being systematic is helpful in asserting yourself. Keep track of when you were assertive. Keep track of when you "blew it." Be honest with yourself. Don't repeat the times you "blew it." Record your assertive responses in a notebook or on 3x5 cards and read them so you'll know your cycle of successes. The track record need not be lengthy. A statement or two describing the situation and how you handled it is all that is necessary. Jotting down how you asserted yourself and using the assertive statements repeatedly will reinforce the behavior until it is natural.

Broken Record, Fogging, Track Record, Imagery, and Modeling are not the only skills that can be used to develop

67

your assertive social and sexual expertise. In my experience with the thousand or more who have completed A-C-T programs, the skills mentioned here are the most effective and simplest to use. When you repeat *any* success you have using assertive behavior, you are shaping your own behavior and building self-esteem. Many of the techniques incorporated in the book have been researched by leading therapists all over the world. I use them! I teach them! They work!

Often people approach me with, "Okay, this is great. I can learn to be assertive, but where do I start?' Start with the expression of positive feelings. Positive feelings are expressions of love, approval and friendship. Don't be afraid to give a compliment or receive one. Most of us have difficulty here. A common situation you may have experienced is one in which you are wearing a new outfit and someone pays you a compliment. They might ask you if it is new. Often, the reply is, "Yes, I got it on sale. It wasn't expensive." Don't put yourself down or become flustered when someone compliments you. If you can't think of anything brilliant to say, a sincere "Thank you" is enough. Reward the complimenter with, "That's a very nice thing to say. I appreciate being told." By rewarding the complimenter with positive feedback, you are shaping behavior and increasing the possibility of hearing positive things. Get over the embarrasment you might feel receiving praise. You are worthy of praise.

One of the things that make us feel *less* worthy about ourselves is giving in when we really don't want to. Often we allow ourselves to be manipulated and wonder how we managed to get hooked. We often hate ourselves for letting it happen. It is important to recognize manipulative techniques. Often these manipulations are expertly and deftly used and our awareness of them escapes us at the time.

Overcoming Manipulations

Manipulations are often messages that are intended to lay guilt trips on you so you will do what the other person wants. For example, if you refuse a request, you might hear someone say, "How can you be so selfish?" "How can you be like that after all I've done for you?" "Don't let me down. Don't disappoint me." Get the idea? You've probably recognized these and more by now with you new awareness. How can you avoid manipulative situations? You can't. But you can cope with them, first by recognizing them.

Begin to build awareness of manipulations. Buy some time. If another person puts pressure on you, it's better to say you need time to think it over than to allow yourself to be manipulated. When the manipulator goes to work, mentally send up a little red flag and watch it go B-O-I-N-G, right to the top of the pole.

If the manipulator is the subtle or devious kind, here's a way not to get trapped. Suppose you had said you would try to bake a cake, pick up the kids, or do something you thought you would be able to do. You find that it is impossible and express that to the manipulator. The manipulator tries to trap you with "You said you would do it, why are you letting me down? Even if you know the manipulator means something else (e.g., "I really don't want to do it by myself"), stick to what he *says*, not what you think he means (trying to guess what someone means will often evoke anger and defensiveness). Repeat what he *said*; e.g. "You are right, I did say I might be able to do it, however, I can't go now. I hope you aren't upset." You don't have to justify or give a lengthy list of excuses. Stick to your guns, persist and repeat. Use the Broken Record. If you are a friend of the other person and *choose* to share how you feel about refusing, do so, that's Assertive.

Hang in there. If you get *silence* when you are making an effort to communicate, you may have to repeat what you are saying or say, "I'm waiting for a reponse." Keep cool and focus on the main issue rather than getting emotionally involved or trying to understand the silence. Don't get into an argument over the silence and lose sight of the main issue. Silence is often manipulative. Often, silence is a way of controlling and shaping your behavior. When someone uses the silent treatment on you, he or she is shaping *your* behavior, preventing you from discussing the issue he or she doesn't want to hear or talk about.

Next time you are having a social encounter, mentally make a note of the manipulative or guilt-inducing words you hear, words like "Why are you so opinionated?" (Aren't *they* opinionated?) Try to distinguish the subtle differences—the obvious statements from the not-so-obvious. A good test for yourself is to see how many of these guilt-inducing expressions you can remember and write them down after the social, business or sexual encounter. In class, we often discuss manipulative expressions. We've come up with literally hundreds. You probably have a list of your own.

Awareness is important. You will have difficulty being assertive if you don't know what's happening until it's all over. Don't get angry at yourself if you miss some things. No matter how perceptive you become with practice, you can't see everything. Concentrate on being more aware of your own environment. If you haven't done so already, now is the time to start thinking about how you will use your new awareness and assertiveness. Let's start getting serious about creating a situation in which you will use assertiveness to be in control of yourself. Practice using the techniques in front of a mirror until you've mastered what you will say and do, even if it is only being able to say "no" when you want to.

If saying "no" to a request makes you feel guilty, express it. You can say, "I wish I didn't feel badly about refusing because you are a good friend, but I do have to refuse now. It puts me in a bind." Don't make excuses. After all, you are entitled to your preferences.

If you decide to work on one particular situation, one in which you will assert yourself this week, concentrate on that one situation and the interaction with the person involved. Don't go in too many directions. Learn how to handle one situation well at a time in the beginning. Build your confidence gradually. (Remember, this is a crawl before you walk method.)

You must be able to take "no" for an answer. If the answer to your request is not one you had hoped for, asserting yourself makes your feelings known. One failure isn't *always*. Don't stop asserting yourself just because you didn't get what you wanted the first time. Asserting yourself helps you to express anger, frustration, requests, etc. in ways that you can build your own communication skills and self-confidence. Asserting yourself helps you direct and take control of your life. One of the objectives is not only improving yourself, but doing it without hurting the other guy. It can be accomplished in ways that can bring you closer together.

When you do assert yourself, it is important to look at the other person. Try to keep eye contact and remain calm while discussing your feelings. It's not easy at first, but you can do it. It will take some effort and concentration until it becomes natural. Once you get in the habit of expressing your feelings without avoiding someone's gaze, you will feel less embarrassed about the real you. The real you doesn't have to hide feelings.

70

How sweet it is to be able to look at another person and say, "I care about you enough not to let this feeling stand in the way. This bothers me (whatever it is) and if I get it out, I can feel closer to you." Be honest and sincere. Concentrate on eye contact and staying calm at first. Making your feelings known, handling your anxiety and trying to keep eye contact are enough verbal and non-verbal skills for starters.

Speaking of non-verbal or Body Language skills, there are many ways to emphasize what you are saying with varied gestures. There are various schools of thought on the use of gestures. It is my feeling and experience that if you worry about what your hands are doing while you are learning the initial skills in Assertive Training, you will be less at ease in communication. Concentration on too many areas at one time makes for less skill. It has been my personal experience that if you look at the other person (eye contact) and express honest feelings, your gestures and body language will be natural and not forced. Let's Get Growing (the A-C-T method) is saying, "Let's get over the up-tight feelings we have. We don't need to add more." Being assertive is reducing anxiety, not adding to your discomfort.

Reducing anxiety is extremely important. When you are able to express that you are nervous, anxious, etc., it clears the air and paves the way for you to state assertively what you want. After practice, when Assertive Behavior comes easily to you, the sense of freedom will be exhilarating. No more will you be bound by the rules that say, "suppress your feelings, don't cry, don't get angry." You will know that you can feel and express those feelings honestly without the frustrating feelings you've had all your life. Expressing yourself assertively is not only feeling better about yourself and others, it can be acceptable to society because it is tactful. You can't beat that combination.

When you are ready to assert yourself, it is okay to move on it. Get ready! Get set! Grow! You don't have to stand rooted to the same square foot on the rug, Physical movement to relieve anxiety might be just what you need at the moment. If you are anxious to a point where you might chicken out of a conversation, you may walk away for a moment. Do tell the other person why you are leaving or that you'll be back shortly. At least the other person won't think he/she has done something to offend you. Get yourself a cup of coffee if you think it will help, or do whatever it takes to make yourself

71

comfortable in order to assert yourself. Relieve your tension so you can become more effective.

Gear yourself up before you enter a situation you decide to handle. Say to yourself, "I will keep cool; I will say. . ." Use whatever ritual works for you. You may have to do some experimenting. In the past, when I have had to call someone about an extremely provoking situation, I've written the words "Keep Cool" in large letters and held the sheet of paper in front of me while engaged in the telephone conversation. I often crumpled the paper into a ball when the anxiety level was high, but nevertheless, it worked for me. Now I just have to visualize the words without writing them down. Find what helps you to say what you want to say. Write down what you'll say. Tape it! Listen to it! Memorize it! Practice it! Say it!

Focus on the person and the communication, not on the anxiety, yours or theirs. They may be as anxious as you are. You will feel better about yourself if you focus on the points you want to make. You won't come away from the encounter feeling frustrated, that nobody understands you, and thinking you must be an oddball. When you share your feelings with another, it is more conducive to improving relationships, whether they are social, business or sexual.

Be aware that sharing your feelings does involve risk. Sometimes you may be turned down (if you make a request), leave yourself vulnerable (if the other person likes to make you suffer), and so on. There are risks involved. Assertiveness is not all smooth sailing once you've mastered it. However, you are the one who will be able to make an active choice rather than wait for the other person to decide in what direction your life should be headed. (For me, the risk is nothing compared to the frustrations I used to experience in not expressing my true feelings.)

You make the choice. You have some influence on your environment. You act instead of react. You stand up and be counted. Doesn't it sound marvelous? It is! Just remember, there is no guarantee what response you'll get. You either take a risk or remain silent and stay in an unrewarding job, have an unfulfilled sex life, a dull marriage, etc. What assertiveness helps you find is the best possible solution to a problem.

72

Best Possible Solution

Communications that have the Best Possible Solution as a goal need several elements to make them work. Here is a little formula devised at A-C-T to help you negotiate, reach a solution or work out a situation. When you are using the formula, follow the steps if you want to see results.

Best Possible Solution Formula:

1. *Talk* = This will include "This is What I Want" (the raise, better conditions, you to communicate with me etc.) and "How I Feel," (about the situations).
2. *Listen* = Allow the other person to express what he wants and how he feels about your request (assertiveness is also being a good listener).
3. *Negotiation* = "How can *we* have a workable compromise?" (To build a better relationship, do a better job, enjoy sex more often, etc.) This step may take some communication to see what is acceptable to both. Stay cool and in control. Focus on the main issue—achieving the goal.
4. *Touch* = Once the bargain is reached, shake hands, touch, or hug. This is a good way to seal the bargin or workable compromise. You have both strengthened the commitment by touching.

My clients (and myself) have used this formula for just about every possible situation imaginable. It will give you direction when you are trying to achieve a solution, and will help you focus on finding it. Act as if you trust the other person. You won't accomplish what you want if your attitude and body language says "I don't believe you." There is some vulnerability involved in acting as if you trust; the other person may not come through for you. However, there is no way to be effective (or assertive) without some risk. Learn to take the risk. Assert yourself and allow yourself to direct your own life. When you control your own life, you will free yourself from the fear that stops you from speaking up or acting in your own best interests.

Looking for an excuse for *not* acting or *not* asserting yourself only sustains your anxiety. Not acting also blocks awareness of the anxious situation you are in. When you are not acting (or speaking up) assertively, you are so wrapped up in the frustration, anger, etc., that awareness of your needs and wants is at a standstill. Sometimes, not acting is a way of punishing yourself for not feeling worthy. For example, "What's the use, they won't listen to me, they won't help." Don't wait until you *feel* you deserve it. Act first! The self-worth will grow along with your confidence.

You will feel worthy if you act on it and see yourself as a person who is assertive and able to achieve, rather than as a passive, acted-upon individual. You will love the new Assertive You! The new awareness will open your eyes to the You you've always wished for, the You that's been buried and frustrated for so long.

Words like awareness, consciousness, assertiveness, are keys to emotional freedom. They can be the "open sesame" to a more productive life. You can achieve, but only if you try. By putting the skills to work for you, with practice, you will acquire expertise of lasting value and a more fulfilled life. You can learn to enjoy life and live it not only more effectively, but successfully as well. Success in living and loving need not be the property of someone else. It can be yours. Remember that improvement in your self-esteem, confidence and attitudes will follow your assertive changes in behavior, especially in those situations you weren't able to handle before this stage of the game. Assert yourself first, watch the emotions (and esteem) take a giant leap upward.

Practice assertive, confident communication using all the skills. The positive results will be your own doing. You will at long last have some influence in your own material and social world. The method outlined here is to aid you in narrowing the gap between what you are and the potential you can develop. Reach and grow!

Behavior change, to be effective, has to be reinforced and practiced. Whenever you do assert yourself and handle a situation in a way that makes you feel good, pat yourself on the back, write about it. It won't hurt to tell someone else about it. If you don't use the skills on a regualr basis, you will revert back to the same old mistakes. After all, the conditioning you've had has been a part of you for some time. If you backslide, don't worry about it. Draw on your personal resources and shape your new behavior by increasing the frequency of successful communication. Even if you don't get what you want all the time, acting positively and assertively will help you become self-directed.

Being human is to have problems, concerns and doubts. Being mature (and assertive) is to try to deal with problems and attempt to arrive at the best possible solutions. Change is healthy. Reexamining old ideas and adding new concepts is challenging. Changing your view-point and attitudes from time to time is to be alive. Being alive is being uncertain part of the time. Success means you are active and trying. Failure demonstrates you are also trying. You have the Know-How. Now Use It!

EIGHTH WEEK ASSIGNMENT

A. Work on increasing your strengths to make you more effective in communicating with others.

B. Practice sharing your feelings with others.

C. Write out the "new assertive way" you will handle a situation. Practice it until you feel it is really You.

D. Go out and try your wings. If it doesn't work, examine how you can modify your handling of the situation so it will work next time. Assertive Behavior is a skill. Like other skills it can be learned by practice. It is acquired slowly with some mistakes along the way. Expect some setbacks, but don't get discouraged. The more you practice, the more you will improve. Don't expect miracles. Do expect less frustration, more awareness and respect for yourself than you've ever experienced before. Work at it! Live it! Enjoy it!

E. Look for assertive models in your own environment. Your lover, mate, employer, friends—all the people you come into contact with. Analyze what makes them assertive. Use Modeling to help you be more assertive.

F. Do use Broken Record, Fogging, Track Record, Best Possible Solution, etc. Develop the Assertive Habit. Whatever you do, Keep on Growing!

Note: Most often, at the end of the program, classes will opt to continue. The length of post sessions vary. They have varied from a single follow-up or post session to several months. The post-sessions are not only to reinforce what has been learned, but to gain new insight, skills and practice in Behavioral Techniques.

The following post sessions offer Sexual Assertiveness and Assertive Punchlines to help you when you need it the most—so keep on Growing.

CHAPTER 9

SEXUAL ASSERTIVENESS

Many of my clients have kidded me about saving Sexual Assertiveness for the last because it is the best part. They also claim that no matter how many people are absent from class at one time or another, *everybody* shows up for this session.

The first statement, about saving it for the last because it is the best part, is, I think, inaccurate. My own feeling is that because the entire subject of sex is so personal and appears to have more hang-ups than other areas, it is easier to deal with once *social* assertiveness is understood and practiced. In teaching people to be sexually assertive, it works well to "save it." By this time, they are less inhibited, more aware of themselves and the effects of assertiveness on their own environment. They are more open to change, less shy, and willing to discuss problems on a more personal level. I don't think it's the "best part," but I do think sexual assertiveness is only one more wonderful facet of the total person.

The second claim is absolutely true. Although the absentee rate is very small in classes anyway, usually everyone does show up for the class on Sexual Assertiveness. Interestingly enough, although shyness and embarrassment are virtually nonexistent at this point in the program, the Sexual Assertiveness session begins with nervous laughter, fidgeting, jokes, and the like. Once we discuss our feelings on the subject and our reactions to it, we begin to settle down. Almost everyone admits to feeling anxiety because she/he doesn't know what to expect.

There are no diagrams, porno flicks, or time for insecurities. We are ready to learn how to apply assertive techniques to sexual behavior. The intent is, as in social assertiveness, to make relationships more rewarding by being more honest and direct. The aim here is to overcome the fears and anxieties that prevent you from enjoying sex.

This is not a how-to-do-it session. For techniques in the sex act itself, I leave those to the Masters (and Johnson). There are many experts in the field who can teach you all about sexual mechanics. My teaching deals with overcoming the no-nos, getting rid of the anxiety and being able to be up front with any relationship. Being able to say "yes" when you want to, and "no" if you feel like it, without guilts and anxieties.

Earlier in the program it was established that the object of Assertive Behavior is to communicate honestly and directly, saying "yes" or "no." When you want to without undue anxiety, without hurting or putting down another person. Sexual Assertiveness applies the same principles. The aim is for two people to achieve the most satisfying relationship possible. Sexual Assertiveness can overcome many problems that might be present in an intimate relationship. It can also make sex more enjoyable.

Some people like close sexual relationships with one particular person. Others enjoy varying degrees of intimacy with several. The number is not important. What is important is the quality and what makes you feel most comfortable. If you allow anxiety to inhibit your actions, and worry about your partner's approval, you are not getting the most out of the sexual relationship. Fulfilling sexual relationships involve honesty as well as feeling.

Women who assert themselves and initiate the sex act have told me that some men find this situation threatening. There is no way of knowing ahead of time. You will have to test to see if the other party can handle assertiveness. Every date or close contact doesn't have to end in sex. At first, even if you only like to lie close, caress or massage one another, that can be an enjoyable experience in itself. The aim is sexual contact.

Sexual contact is often looked upon as a duty in marriage or long-term relationship. After years together, couples often face a sexual slump. Widowed or divorced people often face sexual anxieties either in establishing new relationships or sparking old ones. Whatever problems have evolved, the second half of life must have its own significance. Whatever disillusionment or disparities have occurred in the past, they will often cause conflict in the bedroom and result in open hostility. Instead of looking for ways to correct disparities, often couples will resent, punish, put-down, withhold sex and resort to anger and frustration. Rather than seeking answers in anger (or hunting other sex partners), expectations should be talked about. Talking about them is an important part of being sexually assertive.

Telling your partner what you expect in sex is not easy. On one hand, we are titillated or aroused by TV, magazines, movies, and other media. On the other hand, we are inhibited by conditioning and society. It takes practice to say, "I want to have sex more often with you," rather than devious or damaging remarks like, "You never want sex anymore." or "You're always tired." No one knows what you want until you tell him (or her). If you are afraid or embarrassed to tell someone you want sex, if you've been unable to talk about those things that turn you on, start practicing assertive communication. Learn to say, "I am embarrassed by this, but I want. . ."

Express your fear and embarrassment. It will help to overcome it. Get past the embarrassment and begin to get the most out of sex.

Reducing Anxiety

Despite the fact that two people can be turned on, sometimes one of both will be experiencing so much anxiety, that they act clumsy, say the wrong thing, have premature climax or no climax at all. Anxiety can inhibit what could be a mutually satisfying sexual encounter, while tension can prevent you from handling the situation to the best of your ability.

Identifying anxieties can help a great deal in overcoming them. Talking about the hang-ups, the conditioning and habits that have been with you for all these years, will encourage sharing and closeness. Talk about them, but don't dwell on them. Think and talk about what you both like. It isn't terrible to admit what you like or dislike in sex. Discuss the things that turn you off without a put-down (remember, the put-down is aggressive behavior not assertive). Taling about the turn-offs breaks the ice and relieves tension. Get the uncomfortable feelings out of the way if you want to feel close.

A good time to discuss wants and needs is when two people are physically close. You both need information. Listen to the other person. Put your own anxieties and embarassment aside. (Act independently of your feelings.) Make an effort to understand what pleases your partner. You don't have to agree to anything at this point, but be willing to exchange information to eliminate any problems that might exist. This kind of communication will only bring you closer. The embarrassment will pass. It is temporary. Don't hang on to it.

Reserve the usual snap judgments. Ask questions or make statements to clarify and interpret what each of you wants and expects. It's not easy to do this. We aren't used to being explicit about our sexual desires. However, it does get easier with practice. When both of you understand what you want, the ultimate goal, the deepest exchange of feeling during the sex act becomes possible. It is the difference between being up front and playing the unrewarding game of "he/she should know, I shouldn't have to explain." Mind reading is guessing at best. Don't trust to guessing or luck, not where your relationships are concerned.

Changing Roles

Both men and women have rigid ideas about what their behavior should be. Many are naive and inexperienced regarding sexual play. There is a great deal of scientific information and clinical data available for those wishing to acquire technical skill (see References, Masters and Johnson).

You can learn more about sex to make it interesting and delightful. Now don't panic. I'm not recommending *what* you should do. That will be for both of you to decide. I am suggesting that you do try various things. After all, the same diet does get pretty boring. Passive acceptance of unsatisfactory sexual relationships is reason enough to change. You cheat yourself if you don't learn and try techniques to improve your sex life. Why not enjoy it to the fullest? You don't have to fantasize about being fulfilled. Do somethng about it!

Being fuliflled is possible by being an active participator in the act itself. Women used to be considered the passive partner. Now there is a definite change for the better in attitudes. The idea is that woman is no longer the recipient or passive one to be used for the male's satisfaction. It is no longer considered wrong for her to initiate the sex act and to participate with pleasure. To gain that pleasure, it is necessary to overcome shyness and tell your partner what pleases you. You are also responsible for satisfying him and asking what he'd like. Asking for information you don't know is Assertive. Sex is a mutual act and people often tend to forget it. If the sex act is not mutually rewarding, it can produce tension and rifts. The frustration that results from these rifts can lead to a break-up of the relationship. Sexual problems can often be overcome with more knowledge and assertive communication.

Sex is a meeting of the minds as well as the bodies. Expressing needs prior to sexual play can bring closeness between two people. Closeness can lead to the turn-on and mutual desire. The sexual response is a natural reaction to desire and sexual stimulation (talking as well as physical contact). Don't force the sexual response. Establish the closeness that leads to it. Discuss the things that turn you on (more about keeping it turned on later—Grow On).

If a woman acts as if she reaches orgasm and fools her partner, this leads the partner to believe he must be doing the right thing. Sex cannot improve in this situation. Often the woman is resentful and days later arguments crop up. Don't expect your partner to read your mind. Embarrassment and dishonesty prevent you from resolving sexual difficulty and having what you really want.

Improving and Increasing Pleasure

If you want to improve your sex life, start being aware of the things you would like. Do you want sex twice a week instead of once? Do you want your partner to be more active, to rub your back, perhaps? List your needs and wants. (What do you *like?*) Make your likes known. Determine what you want, when you want it and talk it over with the person or persons with whom you want to improve sex. Enjoy each other. Shape your partner's behavior by reinforcing the things you like.

Most of us are born with the capacity for sexual response, but we are conditioned to think that sex is bad, dirty, perverted, something to suppress. Parents, teachers, church, etc., do a great job of brain-washing us during our formative years. We are taught to be devious rather than to communicate our sexual needs and desires. We never learn how to create a rewarding sex life or to achieve orgasm. We learn how to avoid it. (For example: Q. "Mom, what's the best method of birth control?" A. "Stay out of bed!")

Often in class, we have a discussion about sexual norms. What is "normal?" What are the limits to which we can go in a relationship? Is there a right and wrong in sex? There really is no right or wrong in biology. Right and wrong are cultural, they are taught to us. Brainwashing is an everyday experience. We swallow the myth of the ultimate sexual image—that is, what we are supposed to be. We suffer embarrassment over our sagging breasts, small penises, scars, etc. We expect youth, perfect bodies and the American Dream to last forever. This leads to disappointment and inhibited behavior. It leads to disillusionment. If you think in terms of sex as normal or abnormal, how can you let go when you are afraid of doing something abnormal, perverted, etc.? How can you let go if you think your partner is doing something wrong? Anything is normal if both adults agree to it. It is "normal" for that particular couple.

If you don't believe me, do some research on your own. Research substantiates that just about anything anatomically possible has been accepted somewhere, sometime. Don't impose the word "abnormal" on what you feel or what you want to do. Experts consider sex abnormal when it becomes compulsive, when the individual has no control over sexual behavior.

Blueprints for Change

Pinpoint the sexual behavior you want to change. The goal should be mutually acceptable. Establish a setting that will be comfortable for both of you and conducive to your discussion. If you have a cozy fire in the fireplace and some chilled "bubbly," so much the better.

Don't dwell on the negative or blame your partner. For example, don't say, "You *never* do what I like." Blaming can only leave your partner hurt and indifferent and drive you apart (you want better sex, remember?) Keep the discussion on the specific action you would like to change or add. Focus on problems (if there are any), goals and solution. "What can each of us do to make it better?" If things bother you, express them and encourage your partner to do the same. If you don't know where to start, talk about how often you like having sex. Let the feelings flow. Once you express what you want to change, then you can take action to change it.

Here again, as in social assertiveness, don't trust to luck. *Make plans* to achieve your goals. If you are single and live with children or family, or otherwise have little or no privacy, arrange for a sitter or go someplace where you can both be alone and have undisturbed conversation or technique practice.

Don't look for excuses not to talk to each other if you really want closeness.

If you both try something new and it doesn't work for you—if you don't like it, if it turns you off—it doesn't mean you can never try anything again. Talk about it. Maybe the technique or new action needs modifying to fit your personal styles. When you both decide what you will try, it is important for each of you to be comfortable with that decision. Talk to each other. Listen to each other. Be specific about the things you would like. Be specific before, during and after the act. Instead of saying, "Why do you jump out of bed as soon as sex is over?" say, "I would really like it if you stayed here beside me and cuddled me for awhile." Saying what you like is expressing your feelings—that's Assertive. Reinforce and shape the kind of action you want. Pointing out things you don't like in the other person might put your partner on the defensive.

A word of caution here—your partner may turn you down or be resentful of your new-found assertiveness. There is some risk involved and no way to guarantee what your partner will say and do once you share your innermost feelings. You may be hurt by the other person's reaction. It is my belief that there is no way to achieve a close relationship without sharing your deepest feelings. If you are afraid, it is human. Tell the other person when you are afraid or vulnerable. Ask for help and understanding. This can not only bring you closer, it can give each of you an opportunity to show how much you really care.

Keeping It Turned On

If sex is always the same, experts say this is an indication of a problem that either one is passive or inhibited (see References, Fensterheim and Baer). That statement may be true, however, "passive or inhibited" behavior may not necessarily be a problem. If both people are satisifed with the way it is and both feel fulfilled, close, etc., then passivity is not a problem. The one passive partner may be turned on by the aggressive partner or vice versa. If the sex act is dull or could use a little jolt occasionally, what can you do to spark it or keep it turned on?

Think about options or alternatives in sexual play. Take a bubble bath or sauna together. Set the stage with soft lights, candlelight, music, champagne, or a sexy nightgown. Be imaginative. Try an adult motel, see an X-rated movie, read a sexy book together. Practice new things, discuss sex. Think and talk about things that turn you on. Find out what turns on your partner. Don't put limits on yourself by saying "no" before you try. Increase your pleasure by experimenting. Eliminate the stumbling blocks that prevent you from enjoying each other to the fullest. Think about ways to make sex more exciting. Don't worry about what is *not* happening. Make it happen! Forget the no-nos. Maximize the positives. Show the other person you care. Pleasing yourself and your partner are equally important. Sex is a two-way street.

To have orgasm, let go of reality and experience abandonment. Many fear the loss of control and the inability to regain it. Those fears prevent many from reaching orgasm. It takes getting used to the idea that you can let go. (Get used to it!) Letting go is a way to achieve fulfillment. If orgasm is not reached, don't punish yourself with, "Why didn't I? What happened?" Don't deny yourself a pleasurable experience. You both can cuddle, fondle, kiss, massage, etc., and generally enjoy sexual play. The situation can be an enjoyable experience that might well result in satisfying each other's needs. Relax, forget about no-nos. It can be done, but it takes practice. Try out what you want and see what satisfies you. You won't know until you do. You may not get everything you want, but you can improve the relationship and increase the possibility of getting what you want out of it.

If you really don't feel like having sex, don't do it because you think you should. Many single women have told me that when they date—if the man buys dinner or ... he says he's entitled to a payment of sex. The female, in turn, feels obligated. (I've had the same feelings.) This is no basis for satisfying sex. It isn't necessary to apologize or give in. If you feel pressured, it's okay to say, "I really do want to get to know you. I don't feel comfortable about going to bed with you when I'm pressured. I'd appreciate it if you would stop asking and let it happen. I can't force it. I want to feel turned-on also. Maybe next time."

If you are afraid that by turning down the other person you may lose him/her, be honest about it. Tell your date you want to see him/her again. You would like to allow some time to develop intimacy and you aren't against sex (if you aren't, that is). Express that what you are against is the feeling of pressure or obligation. Say you'd like to make it as enjoyable as possible and you can't under those circumstances. Be Assertive. Be honest and direct. Express what you want, how you feel and ask for your partner's feelings on the subject. Don't put-down and don't allow yourself to be manipulated or put-down. If you allow manipulation, if you let yourself get talked into bed, you won't like yourself. You've been reading, practicing and working at liking yourself for eight chapters. DON'T STOP NOW!

Don't be afraid to change your sexual behavior. Go ahead, be sexy! Develop the total person. Sex is part of you. Assert yourself and work toward the goal of deepest intimacy between two people. The greatest aphrodisiac of all is love. When two people love each other sex is the greatest. Don't sell sex short or take it for granted. It won't always stay warm, loving and explosive without some commitment and participation from you to build a better relationship. Keep turned-on to one of the most rewarding experiences of your life.

The session on Sexual Assertiveness always manages to be the most serious or heavy session in the program. We don't usually waste time on why it is so. We are too busy getting past that. As serious as it does get sometimes, it is not without its humorous side. One of my clients was obviously turned-on by the ideas and conversation in Sexual Assertiveness. He approached me on the pretext that his particular problems would be more easily discussed in private counseling. We scheduled an appointment for the following week.

During the first forty-five minutes of his scheduled hour, he fidgeted and was generally anything but up-front (or Assertive) about his "problems." When I reminded him that it was time to get in touch with his underlying problem, he was finally able to blurt it out. He asked me if I was "into sexual therapy." He felt if he could have sex with me, it would cure his problems (I never did learn what the problems were).

Now, to be Assertive, I must confess, dear reader, counseling is counseling and sex is sex. I never mix business with pleasure. I could not have treated the situation this lightly had the gentleman in question not been a long-standing student and friend. Our relationship in class had been light and so it was easy for me to make the following remarks. I expressed that if sex became my *business* my fees would have to go from what I normally charge per hour to five-hundred dollars per night. (I'd read somewhere that some girls make that kind of money and it seemed like a nice round figure.) His jaw dropped open and we both had a good laugh. He must have given it some thought, although I can't be sure. I haven't seen him since.

Now, Keep on Growing!

CHAPTER 10

PRACTICAL USES

You and Your Environment

By now, if you've been practicing the skills, you are aware of some of the fringe benefits of Assertive Training. Not only is your awareness sharper that it's ever been, but you feel better about yourself than you may have thought possible. You have grown. You have learned a whole wonderful, honest and expressive way of life.

If you are still experiencing some anxiety when you make your feelings known, don't let it stop you. Don't get discouraged if you backslide. Confidence and self-esteem will not come about overnight, especially if you've had a low opinion of yourself all your life. In the beginning, build confidence in easy stages by setting small goals and asserting yourself in situations that are the least anxious. Plan regular assertive communication with people you haven't been able to assert yourself with before. Prepare yourself for these communications and encounters by re-reading your skills, your notes, your assignments, your track record, and so forth. Practice what you will say in the mirror. Use Imagery. Use everything you've learned to help you be more assertive.

The more you assert yourself, the less anxiety you will feel. Help yourself by changing those unrewarding patterns of behavior to ones that are more rewarding for you. You are beginning to peel off the layers of conditioning that have kept the real you hidden. Doesn't it feel good? You are beginning to feel the energy and power within you. You are acquiring a whole new dimension. You may not as yet be the social (and sexual) butterfly or the business executive you've dreamed of, but now you can see the possibilities. Assertiveness has helped you discover your potential as well as given you new communication skills. You can feel the change and you know it can be pretty heady stuff. Others can see the change in you also. You are narrowing the gap between what you are and what you can become.

You've probably also experienced by now that not everyone thinks the new Assertive You is great. If you have been the passive partner in a relationship, if your mate is chauvinistic (male or female), domineering, aggressive, etc., he/she may not be happy with the fact that you can no longer be ignored or pushed around. It may take some getting used to—this new you having a right to an opinion or action in decision-making. Many partners who claim they want mates to be honest or share in problem-solving, decision-making, etc., fight like hell when assertiveness is first practiced. It can happen. You may open a Pandora's box when you change behavior patterns and become more assertive. When conflict does occur, here is the golden opportunity to put your new assertive skills to work.

If your mate, friends, co-workers, or children, complain that the new you is not to their liking and try to put you down, don't fall into the trap. Explain to them that you felt frustrated and unfulfilled before. Tell them you want to grow. Tell them you want to be a more loving, honest individual who can be up-front with any or all of them. Ask them to help you by talking about what they think would be a workable compromise. Negotiate! Communicate! Assert yourself by telling them what you want to accomplish. Tell them how good it feels to be assertive and how good it feels not to be angry and resentful. Teach them to be assertive. Explain that it takes getting used to. You need their love, their patience and their help. You can be effective in your interpersonal environment in ways you had never thought of before. You can help shape their behavior by setting an example.

There's a lot to this assertive business. It isn't something you put on occasionally like a best dress or suit. It's a way of life, an every day honest-to-goodness way of relating to other people. When you use the skills and feel that surge of confidence within you, reinforce the Assertive Behavior with a pat on the back or pat on the cheek. Look in the mirror and tell yourself how sweet was the way you handled that situation. Reward yourself and feel proud. You accomplished what you may have thought impossible. You've had some counter-influence on your environment and it felt exhilarating. The A-C-T Method is concerned both with your behavioral changes and the effects of those changes in your environment.

Most Assertive Training classes, where I received my training, stopped too short. The skills were taught, methods established, practice sessions rehearsed and explanations offered. Some of my instructors offered a word of caution. They mentioned, in passing, the risk involved in asserting oneself. None of my professors offered help once the risk was encountered. The risks need to be dealt with. They are real. What do you say or do in a put-down situation? What do you say to a wall of silence? How do you get through to a person who feels threatened? What can you say to the person who is adept at saying nasty things to you in such a way as to appear cute? How do you handle the manipulator who lays guilt trips on you? What can you do to be your own person, your own best assertive friend without feeling guilty, angry, and hurt when someone disregards what you want? These are some of the concerns of this program. Because you often need answers quickly, because the snappy answers often escape you in difficult and uncomfortable situations, this chapter will include some situations and assertive punch lines that may be helpful. These punch lines are for you to use when you need a comeback. They have come about from my own experience and the experiences of my clients. The answers are never intended to be sarcastic. My clients are encouraged to role-play the answers until they come across cool, low-key, and non-sarcastic to be most effective and assertive.

Situations in which the punch lines are used are factual. Names and locations have been changed to protect the not-so-innocent as well as innocent. They offer alternative ways of handling communication. When answers are rehearsed or role-played in class or private counseling, we focus on more than just words. Close attention is paid to eye contact, voice control, etc. The assertive answer is not only what is said, but *how* it is said. Often the little devil in us crops up and it becomes a great temptation to give a snappy answer that contains an edge or two of sarcasm. Here we often draw a fine line. Even if we don't intend sarcasm at times, another person may receive the answer as a put-down. We never really know how the other person will take what we are going to say. Keeping your voice under control and pleasant will reduce the possibility of another's misinterpretation. However, there is no guarantee what response you'll get either way.

The following examples are situations taken from the classroom. The answers have proven to be most effective in many cases. They are yours to use as you need them:

Situation 1. Vi is an attractive lady who finds that Assertiveness has improved her marriage and social life. She recently served on jury duty and found herself locked up with a hung jury. She was one of the "hold-outs" who disagreed with others as to the final vote. (They really disagreed with *her!)* One of the opposition became very annoyed with her because of her difference of opinion. After some time of trying to change her mind by becoming angry, he resorted to manipulation when all else failed. He flatly asked, "Why don't you give a little?" (It never dawned on him that *he* might give instead.) Vi's assertive punch-line was, "Give a little what?" (delivered without sarcasm).

The punch line is often effective when posed as a question to gain more information or non-acceptance of manipulation. The question lets the other person know you are not accepting the guilt trip he/she is trying to lay on you. It states you have a right to your opinion.

Situation 2. Alice is a homemaker with three active children. She is active in PTA, scouts and is also involved in many community projects. She loves her husband and family and readily admits to being a great cook, but not so great a housekeeper. She is bubbly, creative and able to cope with most problems as they arise, but she had difficulty coping with her husband's put-down type of humor. For example, Alice admits to allowing dust to gather occasionally. Her meticulous husband makes cute little remarks about it and draws hearts or "I love you" in the dust. This annoyed the hell out of Alice. Even though in this case, the assertive punch line is not verbalized, it was most effective in extinguishing the unwanted behavior (writing in the dust, kidding etc.). Instead of reacting and wiping away the dusty "I love you," Alice assertively handled the innuendos by simply writing her message beside the other one—"I love you too." She embellished her writing with hearts and flowers.

Her husband was taken aback; Alice said his mouth dropped down to his navel. He said nothing, but he never did it again. That was another put-down that literally bit the dust. (A perfect exercise in shaping.)

Situation 3. Cindy has anxieties when someone puts her on the spot and asks her to explain something she is doing or saying. Afraid of appearing stupid, ignorant or not knowledgeable with a group of her peers, she often became so tense that she drew a blank or became incoherent. The very thing she feared actually happened. Cindy learned to act independently of her anxiety by controlling it and expressing it. When she started to become incoherent, she stopped herself. She learned to look at her peers as equals, not superiors. She made herself comfortable by saying, "When —— happens, I draw a blank and come across babbling. Often I don't say what I really mean. It comes out garbled and I feel badly." Her assertive punch lines—"Have any of you been in the same boat? How do you handle it? How did you feel?"

By asking the questions, attention was focused away from herself and she was then able to function. Eventually with practice, she had the situation well under control. She learned to answer without redirecting the conversation.

Situation 4. Bea is a pretty, vivacious girl who puts herself down a lot. One of her assignments was to write something good about herself on a piece of paper and post the paper where it could be seen by at least several people. She was to note the reactions, both hers and others. At first she said she couldn't do it. Then she really entered into the spirit of the thing and made a stand-up sign for her desk. The sign was placed on her desk where many of her co-workers could see it as they passed. She had a great deal of apprehension before placing the sign. She worried about what others would say, what she would say, the expected little digs, etc. She decided to take the plunge one morning and put the sign on her desk. Some people made favorable comments. They agreed with the asset she had written on the sign. Others said, "Why are you doing a dumb thing like that?" For the latter, she had a beautiful assertive punch line ready that discouraged further snide remarks. Bea's assertive punch line: "I'm just testing your reaction."

It was brief, to the point and true. Her assertive punch line was effective. She said by the end of the day she felt great about the whole situation. (And proud of her new "asset" and her ability to handle it.)

Situation 5. Debbie has difficulty cutting telephone conversations short. She feels guilty when she has to end a conversation. She invents excuses such as, "the doorbell is ringing," or "the pot is boiling over." She has been particularly bothered by a friend who calls at ungodly hours and talks forever. Debbie's assignment was to keep this reminder beside the phone, "That's all the time I have now, thanks for calling," and hang up. When the calls came at ungodly hours, Debbie had practiced this assertive punch line, "This is not a good time for me. May I call you (if she wanted to) at. . .? Or can you call me back at. . .? I'll have a few minutes then."

If the conversation started to get out of Debbie's control, she was to stop the conversation with these assertive remarks; "I'm starting to get a little uncomfortable because I really don't want to offend you by cutting you short. I do have to say goodbye now."

Later, both friends reached a compromise as to the length of conversations. At this point in time, the situation appears to be under control. Debbie is much happier now that she is handling the situation assertively. She didn't lose her friend as she had feared she would.

Situation 6. Elsie brought up an issue that bothered her a great deal. Her husband responded first with anger and then with the put-down. He told her, "You'll get over it. It's a phase you are going through." Here was a case in which he wasn't willing to accept the responsibility for his frustrating actions and so he attempted to dismiss her. Elsie had learned her Assertive lessons well. She told him it was not a phase; she kept her cool and remained low key. She expressed how she felt about the issue and restated it. Elsie's assertive punch line: "If you refuse to consider my feelings, I'll just have to avoid you until we both discuss how to solve the problem. When you are willing to talk about it without anger or putting me down, leave a note by the telephone. Until then, I don't feel like talking." Elsie was prepared to remain silent and be out of the house all day.

Although the whole problem hasn't been solved as yet, Elsie has told me they are talking about it. She has said she feels less frustrated because the issue is now out in the open. A workable compromise is now in sight.

Situation 7. Connie asserted herself with her lover. She was not happy with his chauvinistic treatment of her on occasion. He treated her like an "inferior female" and she resented it. She was afraid of losing him because she loved him and said he was really a great guy. She felt terribly frustrated when he treated her in this way and decided to talk to him about it. She reported that he acted really "pushed out of shape" when she brought up the subject, but she was prepared. In her best Assertive manner, she reached out, touched his arm fondly and delivered her assertive punch lines: "I get the impression this upsets you and I don't want you to be upset, Honey. I don't want to be upset either and I want us to talk about it." At first this didn't work. He shut her up and threatened to walk out temporarily. Connie was prepared not to be manipulated. Her next punch lines were: "If you walk out, you'll be upset too. There's no point in both of us getting upset, we won't accomplish anything. I'd rather have your help. We need to work this out together." The last I heard, he was trying to understand by listening to her.

Situation 8. Shirley is a pretty divorcee who is sick of men who only offer to take her to bed. She needed some come-back to offer one particular man at her place of her work. The man was married, the office Romeo, and bothered her almost daily with cute little remarks like, "I'm offering my services. After all, a pretty girl like you shouldn't go hungry." On Monday morning Shirley was ready. She had practiced all weekend using Imagery, the mirror and role-playing with friends. True to form, Romeo approached her just before the coffee break and said he was offering his services. He wanted to know when she was going to take him up on the offer. Shirley put on her prettiest smile, touched his arm and used this assertive punch line in honey-dripping tones: "It's so-o-o comforting to know there is friendly neighborhood stud service available. Please leave me your number if ever I decide." Shirley says he has never bothered her since. (She shaped his behavior!)

Situation 9. Bill and Jo had several dates. Jo observed that Bill was turned on, but couldn't figure out why he didn't make a pass. She was turned on by Bill and couldn't tell him. Because she hid her feelings, Jo found out later that Bill was afraid to come on too strong. He was afraid she would be offended. She always acted so "ladylike." Jo was determined to have sex with Bill but didn't know how to broach the subject and maintain her dignity. She was afraid he would turn her down and she might be unable to handle the rejection. The dilemma and frustration were very real. Jo planned what she would say and practiced for days. She was nervous but determined to be assertive. That evening when Bill arrived, Jo, wearing a seductive outfit, had two glasses and some chilled champagne ready. Bill asked what she was celebrating. Jo said she was celebrating feeling good about herself and sharing with him why assertiveness made her feel that way. She then told him she was nervous about what she was going to say, but since that was the way she felt, she accepted it and could act independently of the anxiety. Her assertive punch line: "I've been thinking of how to let you know that you turn me on. I've also been thinking about how I was going to seduce you. I wanted to be clever about it, but all I can think of is being honest with you." Her punch lines were effective. Bill shared his feelings and took her in his arms. Together, they are still practicing sexual assertiveness.

Situation 10. Jack was bothered by his friend's constant borrowing of his tools. He decided to put a stop to the lending because his tools were not at hand when he needed them. When he refused his friend the next time, Jack expressed how uptight he was when he did lend them and how uptight he felt talking about it. His friend used an old manipulative statement to try to change Jack's mind.

92

He said, "You are the *only* one of my friends who has this hang-up about lending something." Instead of reacting as he usually did, Jack's assertive punch line was the result of practicing Fogging. Jack said, "That may be true. However, since I am uncomfortable about lending the tools, I am going to have to say 'no'." Jack only had to repeat it once more to be effective. His friend doesn't borrow his tools any more and Jack feels better about the whole situation.

The discussion obviously didn't damage their friendship. They are still good friends.

Situation 11. Sam is a good-looking young man who attracts the girls. This would be great except for the fact that he could not control his sweating hands and inner discomfort when he was near them. He was miserable. He controlled himself to the point of not shaking hands at all because his own hands were literally wet. He didn't know what to do about the quandary he was in. He had gone through psychoanalysis for about a year without any noticeable improvement. When I first met him, I did not know about his problem and I extended my hand in greeting. He stood rooted to the spot with his arms folded. I was frankly puzzled. I made no issue of it.

Later, after the lecture, I cornered him and expressed (Assertively) that somehow I felt cheated. I wanted to shake his hand. Hesitatingly, he confessed his problem. He told me he needed help. He had never discovered why this happened. I told him I wasn't interested in *why*, but only *how* he could rid himself of the sweaty palms. We didn't wait for the next class or private counseling. Right then and there, I instructed him to assert himself in this way. When there was a girl he wanted to meet. stand close to or touch, for example, he was to tell her he was embarrassed about the problem, express the problem (without apology) and tell her he would like to shake her hand. The next class session, he bounced in. He couldn't wait for the class to begin to tell all of us present that the program was "magic." His sweaty palms had miraculously dried. He then added modestly, "By God, I'm the one who stopped it. That's where the 'magic' really is. It was my repsonsiblity to get it out in the open and express the way I feel instead of being ashamed and hiding." He was so happy about it, he gave me a big hug. (One of my Assertive fringe benefits.)

His assertive punch lines were simply telling the truth.

These are not by any means the only situations where assertiveness comes in handy. The practical use of assertiveness will become more evident as you incorporate it into daily living. Build your own repertoire of punch lines by jotting down remarks you think about *after* the occasion has passed. Jot down successful assertive responses. When, hours later you wish you had come back with the clever answer, write it, memorize it, practice it! Then you will have it ready when you need it. Reinforce it when you do use it. Talk about it, pat yourself on the back. Enjoy it! If we wait for the praise to come from others and it doesn't come, we often feel hurt. Our needs are not being met. They can't be met all the time. To meet those needs, praise yourself and reward yourself in more than one way. Appreciate yourself. Do something nice for yourself. You may find you need less reinforcement from others as you assert yourself more. If the reinforcement doesn't come from others and you have asserted yourself, the hurt may not be as difficult to take. It may even disappear. Become more aware of how important it is for you to feel positively about yourself instead of entrusting that into the hands of others to establish.

You are Important!

There will be times when reinforcement doesn't happen, when you feel down, in a funk and wonder what life is all about. You may even wonder how this A-C-T program can help you then. You've learned how to act, you know the skills but the gut feeling is not the greatest at that moment. How can you think positive when the feelings are so negative? How can you manage your emotions so that you don't feel lousy? Remember way back, early in the book, it was established that changing the behavior changes the emotions? Well here is a little formula that may help you out of the funk you are in. "Positive Experiences=Positive Emotions." What this means for practical use is, redirect your experience to positive ways. Ask yourself, *"How* can I change this negative experience to a positive one so I will feel better about myself? What can I be *doing* instead of reacting? What other options do I have? What would I be *doing* if I weren't blue or depressed, etc.? What magic can I perform to change the way I feel?"

The Beginning

The magic is in the word *doing.* *Action* is the answer. *Act don't React!* Ask yourself "how" or "what" questions. These are questions that lead to action. Action leads to change in behavior and that leads to a change in the feeling. Don't ask yourself "why" questions if you really want to get out of that funk. "Why" questions usually lead to making excuses for not doing something about it. Don't waste the energy. start remembering those things that you did or accomplished to help you feel good about yourself. Repeat your Cycle of Successes and feel good about yourself. You are okay. You deserve to feel good.

One of the ways you can feel good about yourself is to review the goals of Assertive Training. They are aimed at:

    (a) Motivating you to act on *your* needs, *your* desires and *your* feelings. (Use the Fun Jar.)

    (b) Helping you to express your needs, desires and feelings to others.

    (c) Shaping other people's unrewarding behavior toward you without anger or put-downs by setting your limits.

    (d) Establishing better relationships and communication with others.

    (e) Beginning new relationshps.

    (f) Helping you handle situations—socially, sexually or in business without the fears, anxiety or depressions that prevent you from acting in your own best interests.

    (g) Being self-directed, in control of your own life and being fulfilled.

    (h) Getting you to ACT instead of react.

Be one of the Assertive people—honest and direct. Feel less inhibited, less frustrated and simply great.

Assertive people work at being assertive. It's not a one-time starring performance and then resting on your laurels.

Assertive people speak up for their rights and don't build resentments.

Assertive people are assertive with their lovers, their mates, the people around them. They ask for what they want. They don't expect others to be mind-readers.

Assertive people listen as well as speak up. They are considerate and have respect for other people's opinions as well as their own.

Assertive people are not aggressive. They often negotiate and compromise. (It takes two to make a bargain.)

Assertive people accept themselves and their faults. (They are aware they make mistakes occasionally.)

Assertive people are not defensive.

Assertive people are effective.

Assertive people are aware.

Awareness and perception build rapidly when you practice. Sometimes you will feel so perceptive and so sharp, you'll surprise yourself. In class this happens often, but not always as beautifully as it did in one recent session which cries out to be included in this last chapter. As is often the case in class, discussions become intense, personal and lively. One evening we were dicussing the differences in attitudes and mores. When we had discussed attitudes to everyone's satisfaction, one lady asked the $64 question, "What's a more?" The class literally cracked up when a gentleman (with a devilish grin) offered the following explanation: "When the moon hits your eye like a big pizza pie, *That's a-more!*"

On that positive note, you have not reached the end of the program. Learning how to be assertive is actually only the beginning for all us. Now *Grow and Do it!*

The Beginning

About the Author

Born in Sydney, Australia and raised in Canada, Eve Cappello chose the United States as her adopted country. After several years in Ohio and Michigan, she fell in love with Los Angeles and has called it home since 1952.

An exciting and productive career as a singer-pianist for almost twenty years in Los Angeles night clubs has given her an unusual approach to working with the public. During the course of her musical career she raised a daughter and a son, both married.

96

A constant search for self-growth and knowledge led to college enrollment in 1969 where she won both honors and a scholarship before receiving the Bachelor's Degree in 1974. The Master's Degree in Psychology was conferred in 1977 and the Ph.D. in 1978.

Her love of people and psychology has led Eve Cappello to an interesting and productive new career. She established A-C-T Institute, a center for Behavior Modification as a means for self-growth. As a writer, she has authored several courses on self-development using psychological skills. Hundreds of students have completed her courses at the California State University, Dominguez Hills, and the Culver City Department of Recreation.

A Behavioral Consultant in private practice, she has authored *Let's Get Growing*, a book based on her basic eight-week course. Writer of a featured newspaper column, "Behavior and You," in the Hawthorne Community News, she is in demand as a lecturer with organizations and groups like the City of Hope. Her outstanding rapport with audiences stems from many years as a public figure. She loves people and communicates it.

"Teaching people to communicate, to develop potential and handle problems has been one of the most rewarding and fulfilling experiences of my life," Eve states emphatically. Seeking new challenges, doing research and writing, her philosophy is living the self-growth and potential development she encourages in others.

She has developed an Instructor's Manual for Behavior and You as part of the realization of her ambition to train others and eventually spread the good word to many.

REFERENCES

Alberti, R.E., and Emmons, M.L., Ph.D., *Your Perfect Right: a guide to assertive behavior.* San Luis Obispo, Ca.: Impact Press, 1970.

Bach, Dr. George R. and Goldberg, Dr. H., *Creative Aggression: the art of assertive living.* Garden City, N.Y.: Doubleday, 1974.

Bower, Sharon A., and Bower, Gordon H., *Asserting Yourself: a practical guide for positive change.* Adding, Mass.: Wesley Pub. Co., 1976.

Fast, Julius, *Body Language.* New York, N.Y.: Pocket Books, 1971.

Fensterheim, Herbert, Ph.D., and Baer, Jean, *Don't Say Yes When You Want to Say No.* New York, N.Y.: Dell Publ. Co., 1975.

Galassi, Merna Dee, and Galssi, John P., *Assert Yourself: How to be your own person.* New York, N.Y.: Human Sciences Press, 1977.

Gornich, Vivian & Moran, Barbara K. Eds., *Woman in Sexist Society: studies in power and powerlessness.* New York, N.Y.: The New American Library, Inc., 1972.

Kassorla, Irene, Dr., *Putting It All Together.* New York, N.Y.: Warner Books, Inc., 1976.

Kazdin, Alan E., Ph.D. *Developing Social Skills with Behavior Modification: Behavioral Counseling Methods.* New York, Holt, Rinehart & Winston, in press.

Krantzler, Mel, *Creative Divorce: a new opportunity for personal growth.* New York: M. Evans and Co., Inc., 1973.

Phelps, Stanlee and Austin, Nancy, *The Assertive Woman.* San Luis Obispo, Ca.: Impact Press, 1970.

Liberman, R.P., King, L.W., De Risi, W.J. and McCann, M., *Personal Effectiveness: Guiding People to Assert themselves and Improve their Social Skills.* Champaign, Ill.: Research Press, 1975.

Masters, Dr. William H., and Johnson, Virginia, *The Pleasure Bond: a guide to improved sexual intimacy.* New York, N.Y.: Bantam Books, 1976.

Salter, Andrew, *Conditional Reflex Therapy.* New York: Farrar, Strauss & Giroux, 1949.

Smith, Manuel J., Ph.D., *When I Say No I Feel Guilty: how to cope, using the skills of systematic assertive therapy.* New York: Dial Press, 1975.

Watson, David L. and Tharp, Roland G., *Self-Directed Behavior: self-modification for personal adjustment.* Monterey, Ca.: Brooks/Cole, 1972.

Wolpe, J., and Lazarus, A.A., *Behavior Therapy Techniques.* New York, N.Y.: The Pergamon Press, 1966.

GLOSSARY

Terms/Techniques

Acting Independently of Feelings—performing behavior that is effective rather than acting on how one feels. Acting in one's own best interests instead of reacting.

Broken Record—persistent repetition of one's wants, needs, main points, etc., regardless of others' manipulations, arguments.

Fogging—agreeing with the truth or odds of criticism levelled at you and expressing your own wants. e.g. "That may be true, but I prefer not to be reminded that I did make a mistake."

Imagery—imagining how one will act in a particular situation for more effective results. Practice of details of a situation beforehand can alter one's behavior in that particular situation.

Modeling—copying successful components of behavior (body language and words) for more effective results.

Overt—outward expression that is visible and audible, i.e. body language as well as communication. *What* one says as well as the *way* it is delivered.

Role-playing—practicing with another person, those things you will say and do in the actual confrontation.

Shaping behavior—continued use of successful behavior to replace self-defeating behavior. Forming new behavior patterns.

Your Track Record—a daily sheet record to note progress of handling an anxiety situation for one week. Its purpose is to trace effective overt changes in one's behavior.

Workable Compromise—negotiations and compromises are acceptable as long as it means not giving up your self-respect, values and principles. Negotiations in which both parties come away feeling okay.